blue sky | THE ART OF COMPUTER ANIMATION

featuring **ICE AGE** and **BUNNY**

blue sky

PETER WEISHAR

featuring ICE AGE and BUNNY

THE ART OF COMPUTER ANIMATION

HARRY N. ABRAMS, INC., PUBLISHERS

FOREWORD

We arrived at the name "Blue Sky" for our company after it dawned on us that this was where we had started—with a blue-sky idea: extreme, bordering on impractical, and imbued with our naïve expectation that anything was possible.

In February of 1987, six of us decided to pool our savings, buy three computers and a coffee maker, and find out how far we could take our ideas about computer animation. We weren't all that young, but we were enthusiastic. We agreed that if we went through half of the money before we found an investor, we would shake hands and move on with our lives. All the money was gone by the end of the year.

It was a full year after that before we landed our first job. We got it on the strength of a test image, one frame, that took two and a half days to render on all three computers. Ultimately the project would require five hundred frames. We got a loan for another computer and picked up some used equipment from a company that was going out of business. Then, ignoring the omens, we bought some more from another company that was going out of business. We hired an employee and continued to work for free. More people joined to add their own inspiration. They, in turn, inspired more.

Years passed and our little idea was embraced by a growing community of talented and dedicated people from many artistic and technical disciplines. Not only did it become manifest in the world, it grew beyond our expectations.

I hope that the description in this book of our technology and process will interest and inspire you, but understand that what truly makes it work is the spirit of the people who create and use it. Our first movie, *Ice Age*, is a story about finding family where you least expect to, and Blue Sky has become just such a place. It is built entirely on the love of our crew for what they do and their respect and support for each other.

I am incredibly proud of what we have created together and grateful that so many have given so much of themselves to achieve it. These inspiring people have helped me experience for myself the great creative potential inherent in all of us.

After all, the only limit to what can be accomplished in this world is our ability to imagine what is possible. This is the Blue Sky idea, and I promise you that it works.

Chris Wedge
DIRECTOR

CONTENTS

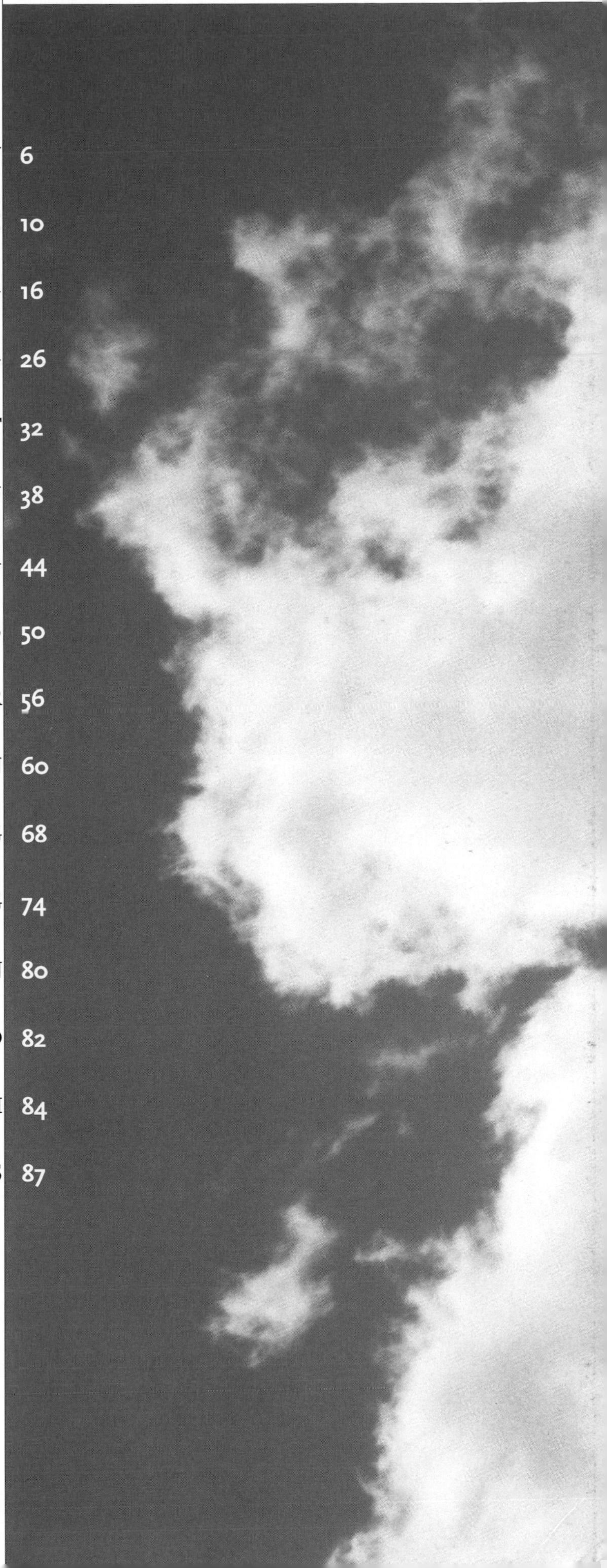

BLUE SKY 6

BUILDING A SCENE 10

MODELING 16

RIGGING 26

3D LAYOUT 32

PRODUCTION AND SET DESIGN 38

TEXTURE MAPPING 44

SPECIAL EFFECTS 50

HAIR AND FUR 56

ANIMATION 60

LIGHTING 68

RENDERING 74

COMPOSITING WITH LIVE ACTION 80

R+D 82

THE RENDER FARM 84

ACKNOWLEDGMENTS 87

Blue Sky Studios' *Bunny* won an Academy Award for Best Animated Short Film in 1998. In the short, which is 7 minutes 15 seconds long, the aging Bunny, baking alone in her kitchen, is annoyed by a moth that flutters around her head, with haunting results. *Bunny* went on to collect another twenty-five international awards for excellence in animation.

OPPOSITE: The feature film *Ice Age*, released in 2002, is a fable starring Sid, a giant sloth; Manny, a wooly mammoth; and Diego, a saber-toothed tiger, who find themselves unexpected allies on a mission to return a lost human baby to its people in a world turning colder. The film's slapstick opening sequence stars an imaginary creature that looks like a combination of a saber-toothed squirrel and a rat: Blue Sky named it a scrat. The scrat became a kind of informal mascot for the studio during the production.

3D COMPUTER ANIMATION IS THE MOST REVOLUTIONARY DEVELOPMENT IN FEATURE FILMS SINCE the introduction of color. The power of the computer has limitless potential to transform the art of filmmaking, giving artists and technicians the tools to bring even the most fantastic visions to life on screen. In the chapters that follow, we'll take you to Blue Sky Studios, in the forefront of this new medium, to show how 3D computer animation is done. Blue Sky, which won the Academy Award™ for Best Animated Short Film for the astonishing *Bunny*, and has just completed *Ice Age,* its first feature film, is one of the places where the future of the movies is taking shape. In the words of *Ice Age* director Chris Wedge, at Blue Sky "people are doing amazing things every day."

Blue Sky Studios was launched in 1987 to create high-resolution computer-generated character animation for feature film. The leaping progress of CGI (computer generated image) animation from the simplistic computer graphics of twenty years ago to the magic that audiences have come to expect today can be credited to the talent, dedication, planning, and genius of a small circle of CGI pioneers. Among the earliest of these were the founders of Blue Sky: Alison Brown, David Brown, Michael Ferraro, Carl Ludwig, Eugene Troubetzkoy, and Chris Wedge.

They brought an amazing range of skills to their fledgling business. Ludwig is an electrical engineer who had worked on the tracking systems for the Apollo mission's lunar module. Troubetzkoy has a doctorate in theoretical physics from Columbia University; he had worked as a nuclear physicist creating computer simulations of nuclear particle behavior before turning to computer imaging. He is one of the pioneers of raytrace rendering, a technique for capturing 3D scenes in the computer with remarkable realism. Ferraro was a performance artist with a masters degree in fine art. He was also an accomplished programmer who worked on some early virtual reality simulations for the U.S. Navy. Wedge was trained as a classical animator and had experience with stop-motion puppet animation. He also had a masters degree in computer graphics from Ohio State University. Most of the group had worked together at a company called Magi, which produced many of the special effects and animations for the groundbreaking 1982 Disney feature *TRON*. Although *TRON* was not a box-office success, it was the first commercial film to feature extensive computer animation, and it is commonly recognized as a watershed event in the history of CGI filmmaking.

From its inception, Blue Sky possessed incredible technical and creative expertise along with a clear understanding of the future of computer animation. What it didn't have was clients or software. For many months the team worked without pay to create the software and develop systems. At this time, Troubetzkoy, Ferraro, and Ludwig developed the core of CGI Studio, which is still today the most sophisticated and advanced rendering software used in production.

Their dedication and sacrifices paid off. Blue Sky Studios eventually set up shop in Harrison, New York, and became one of the highest quality computer animation and effects houses in the country. Its trademark photorealistic rendering and excellent animation brought in such advertising clients as Gillette, Rayovac, Bell Atlantic, and Braun. From the start, the studio produced work that was technically and creatively ahead of its time. As Ludwig recalls, "Many years ago we did a commercial for Braun. We created a computer-generated razor. There was an award we were up for and we didn't end up as a finalist. We didn't understand that, and when we called them up, it turned out they thought we just put some letters in a live-action scene. They said 'Well, 3D letters are not a big deal.'

Blue Sky Studio founders (from left to right) Michael Ferraro, Carl Ludwig, Alison Brown, David Brown, Chris Wedge, and Eugene Troubetzkoy.

OPPOSITE: In the groundbreaking 1982 Disney feature film *TRON*, top, the hero is trapped inside a digital world and forced to play computer games to save his life: this frame depicts a futuristic tank modeled and animated by Chris Wedge. Center, a 1992 Blue Sky-produced TV commercial for Braun featured a computer-generated image of an electric razor was so convincing that experts failed to see that the appliance was not real. Bottom, a TV commercial for Nature's Resource herbal products from 1998 portrayed a ladybug in a natural setting.

We explained to them there was no live action in the scene. The razor and everything was computer generated. This was juried by people in computer graphics. They were judging submissions for their merit in CGI. They were blown away. It has always been our goal, to make rich-looking images." Blue Sky Studios has won many awards for excellence in commercial and film production since then. Its work has also appeared in such feature films as *Joe's Apartment, Death Becomes Her, A Simple Wish, Alien Resurrection, Star Trek: Insurrection,* and *Fight Club.*

Through the years, Blue Sky Studios continued to innovate and experiment. In 1998 the studio released *Bunny,* written and directed by Chris Wedge, who says, "Of anything we've done, *Bunny* was the best model of getting where we wanted to go. We used the same paradigm that we did to start the company: we just sat down and did something we believed in, and that did it for the studio executives. They'd look at the special-effects work and say, 'That's good, but there are 50 to 100 places I could go to get it if I wanted to.' When they saw *Bunny,* they could say, 'Here is a studio of intensely creative people that can pull a movie together and there is no mystery about it.' It was a risk, it was the only thing we've done purely because we wanted to, without any commercial gain in mind, but it paid off bigger than anything else we did."

In 1999, Twentieth Century Fox, which had already invested heavily in the studio, bought Blue Sky outright. With the backing and resources of a major entertainment studio, Blue Sky Studios started production on *Ice Age.* Fox brought in Chuck Richardson, a veteran animation producer whose credits include the cult classics *The Brave Little Toaster* and *Cats Don't Dance.* Richardson oversaw the expansion of the studio from 70 to 170 employees and a move from Harrison to a new facility in White Plains, New York. He helped restructure Blue Sky from a commercial production house to a feature-film company. As Richardson says, "Commercial production is a sprint, features are a marathon." The most difficult part of ramping up for the feature was hiring the right mix of talent and expertise. "People come to you when you have a great project"; the strategy was to "populate the key roles with experience and talent" while hiring the other employees "based on their tremendous potential." The studio brought in pros, such as editor John Carnochan, whose credits include *The Lion King* and *Chicken Run,* and production designer Brian McEntee, art director for *Beauty and the Beast.*

As a wholly owned division of Fox Feature Animation, Blue Sky Studios has maintained its quirky style and commitment to technical innovation through research and development. *Ice Age* exemplifies the state of the art of computer animation today. The characters have the look of stop-motion puppets, combined with the fluid and believable animation only possible with CGI. The lighting and sets are outstanding in every magnificently rendered frame.

Although Blue Sky Studios has its own innovative ways of doing things, almost every major studio follows many of the same basic steps to create 3D computer animation.

Whether a feature is planned for traditional 2D cel animation or all-digital 3D computer animation, much of the pre-production process is the same: scripts are still developed in the traditional manner, hand-in-hand with hand-drawn concept sketches and storyboards. We will begin at the point where the characters and sets are brought into the computer, covering the steps necessary to bring *Ice Age* to the screen, with occasional detours to other Blue Sky projects, particularly *Bunny*.

What you need to keep in mind as you read this book is that in 3D computer animation, a fully 3D world is created in virtual space and then recorded by a virtual camera, which produces the images you see on the screen. This means that most characters, props, and sets—called models—have to be built in 3D. The process by which this virtual 3D world is turned into the 2D image that gets printed on film is called rendering. Needless to say, modeling, animating, and rendering in 3D require highly sophisticated software, massively powerful computers, and—most of all—very skilled artists and technicians.

Like all artistic tools, 3D computer animation can be used to express many different visions. When Blue Sky launched *Ice Age,* it had already mastered the art of photorealistic computer animation. The studio's work had seamlessly appeared in many films, side by side with real sets and actors, and it had also created in *Bunny* an animated fable with a naturalistic visual style. *Ice Age* is deliberately not naturalistic. As in a satisfying children's picture book, the sets and characters look believable within their own world, but they are clearly not trying to look "real." Whatever worlds the artists at Blue Sky conjure up in the future, they will be building on the basic concepts, skills, and tools described in this book.

THIS foldout charts the evolution of a single scene of *Ice Age,* from conception to final frame. In this scene, Manny, a wooly mammoth, and Sid, a sloth, are standing on a riverbank, watching as the human Nadia—who has leapt off a waterfall to escape from Diego, a saber-toothed tiger—struggles to save her baby, Roshan. Below is the scene as it appeared in a very early watercolor sketch by the production designer. Such sketches, created in pre-production, help to establish the look of the film, from characters and sets to color and lighting. Opposite is the final scene as it appears in the movie. In between, characters are modeled and animated, sets are built, special effects are added, and the scene is lit and "filmed"—all in the computer.

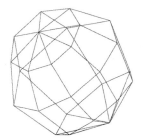

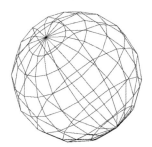

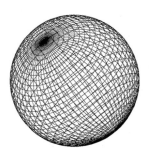

IS ONE OF THE FIRST STEPS IN DIGITAL PRODUCTION FOR A CGI

feature. Often—as in the case of *Ice Age*—modeling commences work during the pre-production phase, even before the film has received an official green light from the studio, when artists begin to develop hand-drawn concept sketches of characters and sets. Blue Sky Studios employed about ten full-time modelers, whose task it was to produce virtual 3D models for the actual film. They came from various backgrounds, but most had experience in traditional sculpture or industrial design. The group worked as a team, with everyone jumping in as needed. Although there were no specialists per se, the more difficult complex character modeling usually went to the more experienced staff.

A model is any 3D object that will appear in the film. Some models, especially the lead characters, are highly complex. Others, for example background items on the set that aren't props and therefore won't be handled by one of the characters, are simpler but much more numerous. All models must be "built" from scratch as 3D forms that can be seen from different angles within the virtual space of the computer. The modelers work on what appear to be wire sculptures inside the computer. They can also view the models as monochromatic 3D forms. Later, the sculptures will be covered with textures, and the ones that move will be given jointed skeletons so that they can be animated.

Inside the computer, points in space are mapped along three intersecting perpendicular axes. The software gives a numerical value for height (the distance from the intersection along the X axis), width (the distance from the intersection along the Y axis), and depth (the distance from the intersection along the Z axis). The artist uses these X, Y, and Z coordinates to locate points on the surface of an object. The points in space describe the general shape of the object, and the software draws lines to connect them. The intersecting lines will serve as the ribs for the surface of the model—like chicken wire under papier-mâché. The software that creates 3D objects by describing their surfaces is known as a "surface modeler." The models created in a 3D program are often simply referred to as "the geometry."

There are two basic methods of creating a model in the computer: one uses polygons to describe its surface, and the other, splines. A 3D object made of polygons is constructed very much like a brick house, with each polygon butting up against another. The geodesic domes designed by Buckminster Fuller are classic examples of 3D structures made from flat planes, in this case triangles. Spaceship Earth at Disney's EPCOT is another real-world example. A sphere made in a polygonal modeling program looks very similar. In a polygonal modeler, the smoother the surface required, the more polygons are needed. Imagine a geodesic dome made from large triangles—the surface hardly approximates a smooth curve. The same dome constructed with more and smaller triangles will have a much smoother surface. Indeed, if the triangles are below the threshold of human vision, the surface will appear to be a true curve.

As these diagrams demonstrate, the more polygons that are used to model a sphere, the rounder it becomes. An enormous number of polygons are required to form a sphere that appears to be smooth.

In pre-production, artist Peter de Sève made many concept drawings to establish the appearance of the main characters of *Ice Age*. This sketch includes Sid, a giant sloth; Manny, a wooly mammoth; Diego, a saber-toothed tiger; and the human baby, Roshan.

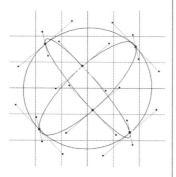

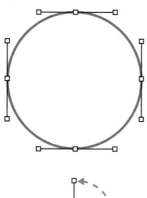

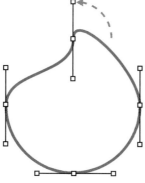

Using splines, a smooth sphere can be modeled with far less geometry than with polygons. As the top diagram shows, all that's required is three circles that intersect at six vertices. At each vertice, there is a control handle that the modeler can use to change the curvature of a spline. The second diagram shows what happens to a circular spline when a control handle is moved.

A spline modeling program creates surfaces in a different manner. Think of a dome tent. Each rib, or spline, of the tent curves along an axis. The ribs are positioned at an angle to each other so they intersect at the apex of the curve. The skin of the tent is then stretched over the ribs to create the 3D or "solid" shape. The dome tent is a very efficient form of shelter because its underlying structure is only a few simple ribs. In 3D software, the same is true. A modeler can describe an entire sphere with three circular splines, one at the equator, and two at 90 degree angles running longitudinally. The computer will then calculate how the surface will stretch over the splines.

With splines, a modeler can make a 3D object using very few points. In CGI, a model that is very efficient is often known as a "light" or "inexpensive" model. Light models generate smaller files and are easier to animate and work with. Polygonal modeling does have its advantages, but generally, when it comes to making smooth surfaces, polygonal modelers generate "heavier," more data-intensive geometry.

Many simple models can be created in the computer with just a rough 2D sketch as reference. However, when creating a complex organic model, the artist often takes the trouble to create a small physical sculpture known as a maquette. For *Ice Age,* Blue Sky's lead modeler, Mike DeFeo, and his team refined the proportions of the main characters (most of which were designed by Peter de Sève) using Super Sculpey modeling clay. Each maquette was approximately 14 inches high. Once the character design was approved, the sculptures were prepared so the coordinates of the surface could be read into the computer. Blue Sky used a Microscribe ARM to digitize the models. First, a grid is drawn over the entire surface of the model with a marker, for visual reference. Then, the artist touches the maquette with the pen on the arm at each point where the grid lines intersect. When the pen touches the hard surface, the X, Y, and Z coordinates of that spot are recorded in the computer's virtual space. The coordinates become recorded points (called vertices) in the modeling program. Blue Sky Studios uses Rhino as the interface for the digitizing process, and Maya, the state-of-the-art software from Alias|Wavefront, for modeling and animation. Maya, preferred by most computer animation studios, is arguably the most sophisticated and complete modeling and animation software on the market. It can create models using either splines or polygons, depending upon which the modeler selects.

The software takes the surface data—the vertices—collected by the ARM and connects them with a web of splines. These splines run in two directions around the object, to form a 3D grid very similar to the imaginary longitude and latitude lines used to measure distance across the surface of the earth. In 3D, the longitude and latitude are known as "U" and "V" directions, respectively. Once the splines are generated, the artist "skins" a surface between them. In theory, the resulting surface should be an accurate digital recreation of the original maquette. If it were only that easy. In practice, digitizing is just a jumping off point for many weeks of work. The original maquette usually takes about three weeks to complete. Digitizing takes about one day, which saves about a week of production time

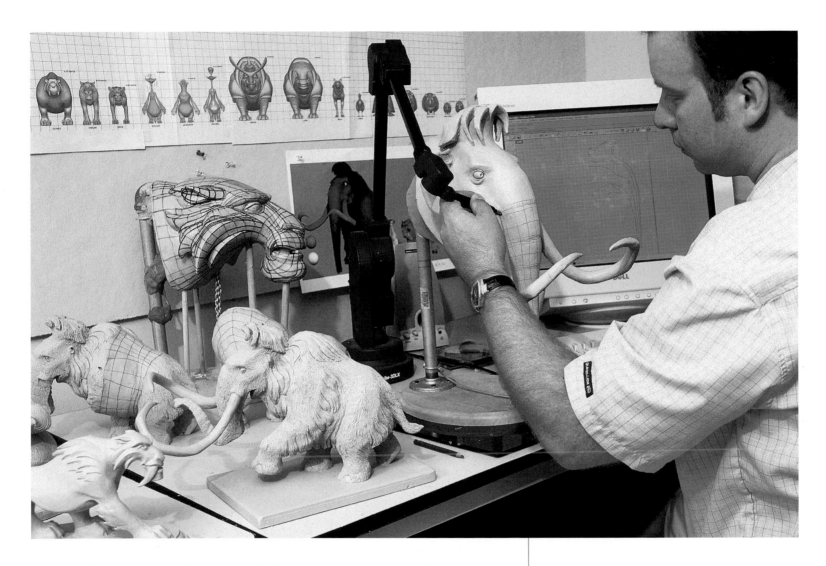

Using a Microscribe ARM, modeler Mike DeFeo 3D scans the maquette of Manny's head. The digital model is beginning to take shape on the screen behind him.

over straight computer modeling. After digitizing the maquette, the artist can expect to work for about two and a half months to complete the character.

Here's the problem. A spline modeling program will draw a smooth curve between the vertices by default (this is why only six vertices are required to define a sphere). For example, a curve connecting three vertices would look more like a bell curve than a "V," even if the surface of the model is actually creased at the center point rather than gently curved. On a 3D model, the bell-curve effect will generate unintended dips and bumps in the surface. If the modeler adds more splines, the bumps become smaller, but the model becomes heavier and harder to work with. Maya offers a sophisticated kind of spline known as a NURBS (for "Non-Uniform Rational B-Spline"), that has control handles off the curve. The modeler can shape an individual curve by manipulating these handles in 3D space, and will spend literally hundreds of hours on a complex organic form pushing and pulling the control handles (or control vertices) on the spline curves in order to create a model that is both efficient and accurate. A master painter creates art with as few descriptive brush strokes as possible. A master modeler creates a virtual sculpture with the same kind of artistry and finess.

ABOVE: These three images show how Blue Sky Studio's custom software called Suction Cup works to join shapes together, in this case a cylinder and a sphere. Suction Cup "deforms" the tube so it appears to be attached to the sphere. When both objects are the same color, they appear to be part of one seamless surface. Suction Cup is especially useful to help model complex forms like human hands.

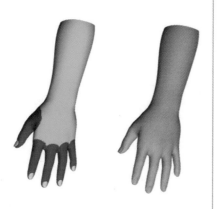

To create a complex model, the modelers use multiple NURBS surfaces attached to each other. Imagine modeling a human character. The torso might have the "U" splines running in the direction of the waist and the "V" splines running from the shoulder to the pelvis. To pull an accurate arm out of the torso would require a large number of splines in the shoulder area. Since the curves go all the way around the surface, this would add density all around the torso. Then try to imagine adding a hand and fingers. The smaller appendages would require an even denser grid. The model would become virtually unworkable. Instead, a modeler will make the arm as one shape, and the palm and the fingers as their own separate NURBS shapes. The biggest challenge is taking all of these separate shapes and making them appear as if they are part of one seamless surface. To do so, the modeler must achieve "surface tangency" (the smooth transition from surface to surface) between each piece of geometry. Skilled modelers can spend months working on surface tangency problems for a main character.

Blue Sky Studios has proprietary software that works with Maya to solve this problem. It is an elegant and simple-to-use tool written by Maurice Van Swaaij, aptly named Suction Cup. Using Suction Cup, the modeler selects two objects that should appear as one surface, and one of the surfaces automatically deforms around the other with accurate tangency. For example, in the model of Manny, the wooly mammoth that is one of the lead characters in *Ice Age*, the front legs are created as one continuous surface. The hindquarters were also modeled the same way. The body of the character is then suction cupped between the two. For complex faces, protruding noses and ears can be suction cupped onto the head, saving geometry and time.

NURBS are not the ideal solution for every shape. For example, jagged rocks, with their sharp corners and flat planes, are better represented with polygons than splines. One of the challenges of polygonal modeling is using enough polygons to create an illusion of detail while avoiding a very high polygon count. If you play video games, you will notice that the sets (and even the characters) are often created with large flat shapes. This is because the game designers needed to keep their polygon count very low in order to speed up screen redraw and to accommodate the limitations of your computer's processor. As game machines become more sophisticated, polygon counts increase and the geometry becomes more smooth. Game players will accept polygonal artifacts; moviegoers would find them distracting. Since film resolution is much higher than a game, the polygon count would have to be astronomical for polygons not to be visible in objects projected full screen.

Blue Sky Studios has a proprietary software tool called Epiderm that addresses this problem. With Epiderm, the artist creates the polygonal model, adding detail into the desired areas and leaving some of the less descriptive parts of the model with just a few polygons. The modeler then applies Epiderm, which will smooth out the surfaces.

Here, Manny the mammoth from *Ice Age* is seen first in a colored version that shows the separate NURBS surfaces that make up the model; then as a monochromatic 3D form in low resolution, without his fur; and finally as he appears in the film.

Like an extra, secondary computer models can appear in many different productions without anyone recognizing them. Blue Sky Studios was commissioned to create talking fish for the season finale of the first season of HBO's "The Sopranos," above. One of the fish was used again in *Ice Age*, right. The coloring was changed so it was not as photorealistic.

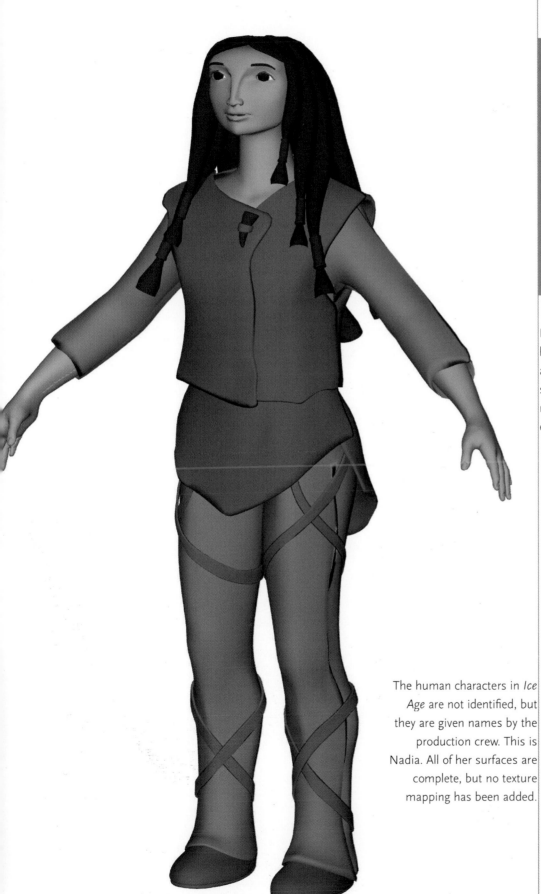

Like a buyer inspecting a horse, a modeler will check a character's teeth to make sure the inside of the mouth will look right in extreme poses.

The human characters in *Ice Age* are not identified, but they are given names by the production crew. This is Nadia. All of her surfaces are complete, but no texture mapping has been added.

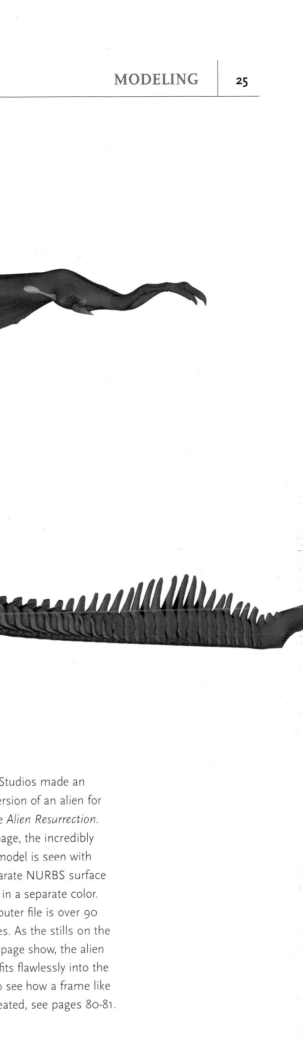

Blue Sky Studios made an all-CGI version of an alien for the movie *Alien Resurrection*. On this page, the incredibly detailed model is seen with each separate NURBS surface rendered in a separate color. The computer file is over 90 megabytes. As the stills on the opposite page show, the alien creature fits flawlessly into the movie. To see how a frame like this is created, see pages 80-81.

AFTER A CHARACTER MODEL IS REFINED AND APPROVED, IT MUST BE "RIGGED" SO IT can be posed by the animators. In computer animation, the rigger creates a series of controls that determines the nature of the character's movement. This is the interim step between modeling and animation. Without a rig, a computer-generated model is nothing more than a rigid sculpture, and the only way to animate it would be to literally remodel the geometry at almost every frame.

The first step a rigger takes is to build a skeleton inside the model. In 3D computer animation the skeleton does not support the structure; it is only used as a guide for movement. By default, the skeleton is not a "renderable" object, so it will not be seen by anyone but the artist working on the file. The skeleton is comprised of a series of connected rods with a pivot at each end. The rods are known as bones, the pivots are appropriately called joints. The rigger can limit the rotation of each of the joints so the skeleton does not move in an unnatural manner. A knee joint of a human figure might be constrained to rotate only along a single axis, that is, forward and back but not sideways. The knee can then be set up so the rotation has a limited range. A knee can go from a fully extended straight leg to the point where the heel touches the character's posterior. If a character's knee could bend all the way forward (or wiggle from side to side, for that matter) it would look like it was broken. At Blue Sky Studios, joint limitations are used sparingly. Instead, the animator uses common sense and instinct to decide what works for the animation.

The simplest way a character can be moved is by rotating the joints of the skeleton one at a time (like manipulating a poseable toy action figure or stop-motion model); such movement is known as forward kinematics (FK). Kinematics is term for the way things move. For example, a machine with gears uses forward kinematics, since motion is transferred "forward" from gear to gear. In some instances, like rotating a shoulder on a human character, forward kinematics is the best and most straightforward solution for a rigger. However, animations done with FK are not always the most efficient method of emulating fluid or realistic character movement.

The solution that many character riggers use is called inverse kinematics (IK). With inverse kinematics, the skeleton is rigged with a series of "IK solvers" that work like a network of tendons (puppeteers' strings are sometimes rigged to work this way as well). When the artist pulls on the end of the tendon, the attached bones move. For example, when rigging the bones on the leg of a human figure, an IK solver might be connected directly from the hip joint to the ankle joint, still leaving the knee joint in the middle with same rotation constraints as described above. When the end of the IK solver (known as the "end effecter") is moved, the entire foot and leg move from the ankle, effecting the rotation, but not the location, of the hip joint. With IK rigging, the knee will have a natural bend when the animator moves the ankle toward the hip. In this manner, the animator can also move an entire series of joints just by grabbing one handle on an IK chain. Although it can be rather complex to set up, IK simulates a more natural kind of movement. Imagine trying to pick up an object

OPPOSITE: An X-ray view of the human baby from *Ice Age*, called Roshan, shows his internal skeleton. The wire shapes around the model are the handles the animators use to pose the figure.

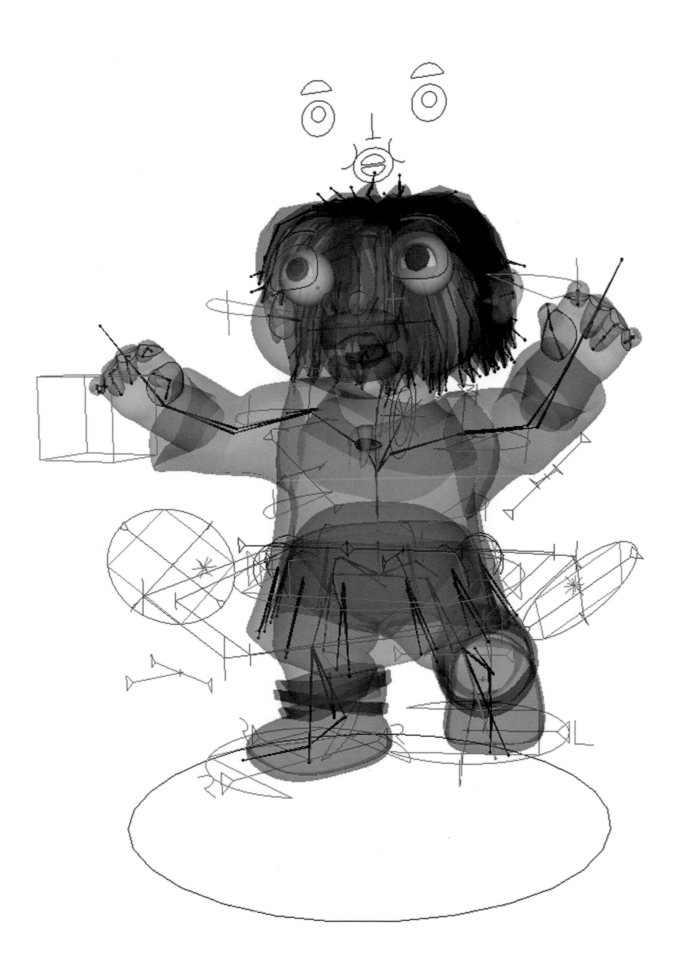

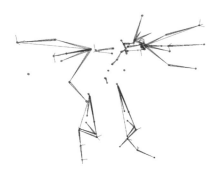

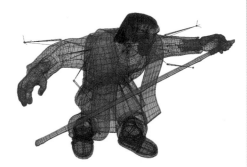

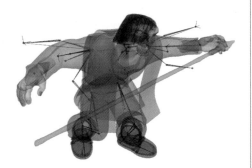

THIS PAGE: The skeletal rig for one of the human character models in *Ice Age*; a wireframe view of the model over the rig; an X-ray view of a low-resolution version of the model; and the final model in the pose set by the rig.

OPPOSITE: The skeletal rigs of two tumbling rhino models from *Ice Age* (note the extra spur extending into the midsections of the rhinos that controls the follow through of the jiggling stomachs as the characters move); a wireframe view of the same shot with the rigs visible; the shot rendered with color and texture; and the final frame as it actually appears in the film, with blurring added to moving objects to emulate the look of an image taken with a real camera.

that is just out of reach while you are in a sitting position. First you would move your fingers toward the object, then bend your hand, and then maybe straighten your arm. If it is still out of reach, you may turn your shoulder and then eventually bend at the waist to lean your torso toward the object. It is almost as if the tips of your fingers are pulling the rest of the your body toward the object. This is a very close simulation of inverse kinematics.

For *Ice Age,* the riggers actually used three skeletons for each of the main characters. Each skeleton effected the character model in a different way, one for forward kinematics, one for inverse kinematics, and one skeleton for attaching the geometry. The riggers make the skeletons work together by writing custom scripts, known as "expressions," using MEL (Maya Embedded Language), a computer language similar to C++ that works within Maya. With MEL, a rigger can write a set of expressions to give a character distinct attributes. For example, the rotation of the shoulders can be linked to the hip rotation (that is, a MEL script would say something like "if joint 4 rotates in x direction then joint 5 rotates a certain amount in another direction"). The custom script will give the character a distinct way of moving. For example, the character's torso might swing as he walks.

Subtle rigging can help the animators work with a character later. Every character animator, from traditional 2D cel animators to 3D computer animators, is concerned with creating a "believable" character. Even if the character is something as unlikely as a talking giant sloth walking upright on its hind legs, it will be believable if it seems to have weight and presence in the scene. One way to give the character a sense of weight is to "plant" the feet. When the foot is planted it stays in one place until the next step. In CGI the rigger will usually set up a "foot roll" expression that places a pivot point at the ball of each foot. When the character steps heel to toe, the foot will bend and roll (or pivot) around the ball of the foot. The ball of the foot is then controlled so it stays on the ground until the animator intentionally moves it. This way the character will usually have at least one foot on the ground as it walks, just like in real life.

The riggers can set up characters so that movement is coordinated over their whole bodies. Before rigging the saber-tooth tigers in *Ice Age,* the riggers first studied the movement of big cats. The tigers' skeletons were then set to enable the model to crouch, leap, and walk in a feline manner. When a tiger takes a simple step, a great deal more happens than just a leg moving forward. His tail may wag a bit, his pelvis will rotate, his back may curve, and various other parts of the body will shift to compensate for the redistribution of weight.

Before all of the expressions and constraints are created, the rigger must attach (or "bind") the skin of the character to the skeleton. Blue Sky Studios uses a software feature in Maya called Smooth Bind. Smooth Bind will automatically calculate how the surface will bend around the skeleton. While Smooth Bind may solve about 80 percent of the calculations without a problem, there is still a great deal of work to be done. While a character may look great in the original bind pose, various extreme positions may cause major problems. For example, if an animator were to fully extend the forearm of one of the cats, the model might "tear." Tearing occurs when two tangent surfaces are pulled to the limit and one of the surfaces separates from the other, leaving an open hole. To avoid tearing, the rigger may consult with the modeler to add more detail into the problem area, or perhaps add weight to the control points to create a stronger bond between the surfaces. If the same arm were to be bent in an extreme position, other problems may occur with the geometry. If you bend your own arm to the point where your forearm and biceps touch, you'll notice that your arm actually changes shape, compressing at the inside of the joint and bulging at the biceps. In 3D, the geometry of a smooth bound arm will bend more like a rubber tube. Also, if the arm is bent too much, the geometry on the insides of the elbow joint will intersect. To solve these problems, the riggers use something called a deformer. In Maya a deformer is a control that changes the shape of the model. One very popular kind of deformer is called a lattice. A lattice is a segmented box that envelopes the geometry. The more complex (or dense) geometry on the surface of the character can be controlled by manipulating points on the lattice. A model of an arm might have two or more associated lattices. One lattice would be placed at the joint to prevent intersecting surfaces. Another might be placed at the biceps to bulge the surface when the arm bends. A fully rigged character will usually have about twenty or thirty deformers. The riggers at Blue Sky tend to use a kind of deformer called an influence object on their characters. An influence object is kind of like an extra bone on the skeleton. The rigger can control the surface of the model by adjusting the position of the influence object.

Talking characters require a specialized type of rigging so their mouths can form the correct shape for spoken sounds. This is called "lip sync." Language is broken down into key sounds known as phonemes. The animation technical assistant must place the corresponding mouth shape at the right point in the animation so the character appears to make that sound. The sound "mmm," for example, is a phoneme formed by pressing the lips together. A version of each character is saved with the lips in that position. The animation technical assistants at Blue Sky Studios start with a finished facial rig for the character. This means

Occasionally the storyboard calls for a pose that literally "breaks the rig" by bending it much more than the rigger intended. This shot called for Manny to lean his face close to the ground without bending his front legs, an impossibility for a mammoth. To make the shot possible, Manny's off-camera hindquarters and legs were up in the air, as if he was balancing on his tusks and front legs.

that all of the controls are already set up so the technical assistant can move the parts of the face by using a set of sliders. Once the technical assistant has formed the correct shape for a phoneme, the pose is saved into the poseToolbox. The poseToolbox is a proprietary piece of software written by Austin Lee that enables an animator or technical assistant to save any character pose in any scene and export it to another. This tool helps with continuity between scenes and provides a library of useful poses. The lip sync artists then import a rough soundtrack into Maya. The digitized sound can be displayed as a waveform underneath the model window in the Maya interface. A waveform is kind of like a seismograph output. A loud sound makes a hill (or wave), silence produces a flat line. The technical assistant "scrubs" through the soundtrack by moving a cursor along the waveform diagram. At the appropriate points, the phoneme mouth shapes are imported.

Almost every character produced at Blue Sky Studios is capable of asymmetrical facial movement. This enables the animator to raise one eyebrow, curl a lip, and emote in a more natural manner. The technical assistant can set the character to "morph" from one shape to another with a smooth transition. In Maya the tool that achieves the gradual transition between shapes is known as Blend Shape. Using Maya Blend Shape, the technical assistant can use a set of sliders to add a percentage of one shape on top of another. For example, a character can look 50 percent surprised while raising one eyebrow 30 percent and saying the "r" sound. Once the character appears to be speaking, the lip sync technical assistant's work is done. The file is then sent to the animators, who will add more expression and appropriate facial movement to coincide with the character's emotions and the tenor of the scene.

Blue Sky Studios employs four full-time riggers, including the lead technical animator, Mark Pirretti. During the height of production that number might be increased to about nine individuals. Blue Sky is unusual in that many of its full-time riggers have experience as character animators. After the bulk of the rigging is completed on a project, many of the riggers will move over to the animation team.

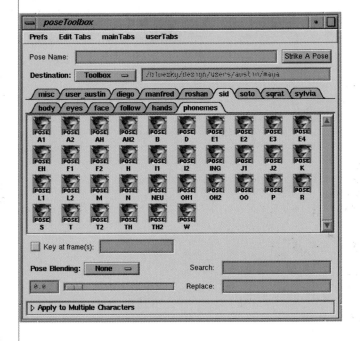

The interface for the poseToolbox, above, shows the mouth positions for articulating different phonemes for Sid. Note the rows of tabs, identifying folders for different characters or animators' work, with subfolders for body poses, eyes, faces, hands, and so forth. A library of poses is created for each major character in a feature film. Four of Sid's lip sync poses are shown below.

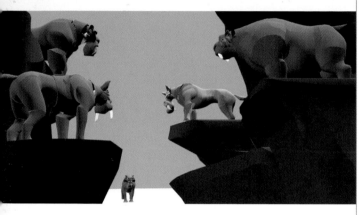

A sketch from the *Ice Age* storyboard (top) shows saber-toothed tigers perched on outcroppings of rock overlooking a pass where another tiger is approaching from the distance. A frame from the 3D layout animation of the same scene (above) reveals that the layout of the rock has been changed significantly to accommodate the movement of the animation and enhance the composition, but the general camera angle, position of the tigers, and feel of the shot remains the same as planned in the workbook. Overleaf, the final render as it appears in the film. The models have been fully posed, the lighting has been refined, and the set has been detailed.

THE RIGGED CHARACTER MODELS NEED A STAGE UPON WHICH TO PERFORM, A WORLD in which to move. The creation of this world begins in pre-production, when production designers begin to envision the locales of scenes and storyboard artists sketch out the action. 3D layout is the phase where these hand-drawn set designs and storyboards are translated into 3D computer animation. The general public will never see the artwork produced by a 3D layout artist. It is used as a guide and master file for the modelers who will make the final environments. Blue Sky Studios employs five full-time 3D layout artists for *Ice Age*, who are led by Rob Cardone, a Disney veteran who was an artist for the Academy Award–winning Deep Canvas effect used on *Tarzan*. The 3D layout artists will work through almost the entire production process, interpreting each sequence into 3D as it "goes through the pipeline."

In pre-production, each sequence is storyboarded by hand. A storyboard is like a comic book of the final film that shows the significant shots and camera movement. Storyboards serve as a guide during the production of a film. Since artists and technicians must painstakingly produce every single frame of an animated film, the storyboards for animation are much more detailed than those used for live-action movies. An animated feature will have thousands of storyboard drawings. Once the storyboards have reached a certain level of approval, the key drawings are assembled into a workbook. A workbook page contains panels from the storyboards with camera angles, mechanics, and descriptions of the action.

3D production starts with a large blue-book meeting attended by some of the animators, layout artists, technical directors, producers, and the directors. In this meeting the directors act out and explain the scenes, using the workbook as a guide. In the blue-book meeting, the director can communicate the intent of the scene, as well as many of the details that cannot be expressed in story panels. In addition to the information from the meeting, and the workbook, the 3D layout artists also rely on the story reel to help them interpret a sequence. The story reel is a video produced by the editors with a scratch soundtrack and storyboards as visuals. From the story reel, the 3D layout artist has a better sense of the intended timing and the flow of the story.

Each animated film is broken up into sequences; a sequence is comprised of a series of shots. In film and TV, each time the camera cuts to another view, it is a new shot. A feature film like *Ice Age* has thousands of shots. Each sequence is assigned to a layout artist. It is his or her job to roughly block out the proportions and the position of the models for the set, as well as the movement and position of the characters and cameras in 3D. The layout artist then produces a rough animation that corresponds to the hand-drawn workbook.

This is a crucial point in the realization of a 3D animated feature. While the storyboards may tell the story beautifully, they do not include details about the set and characters, such as "three foot high rock, twelve feet from the camera with character one foot to the left."

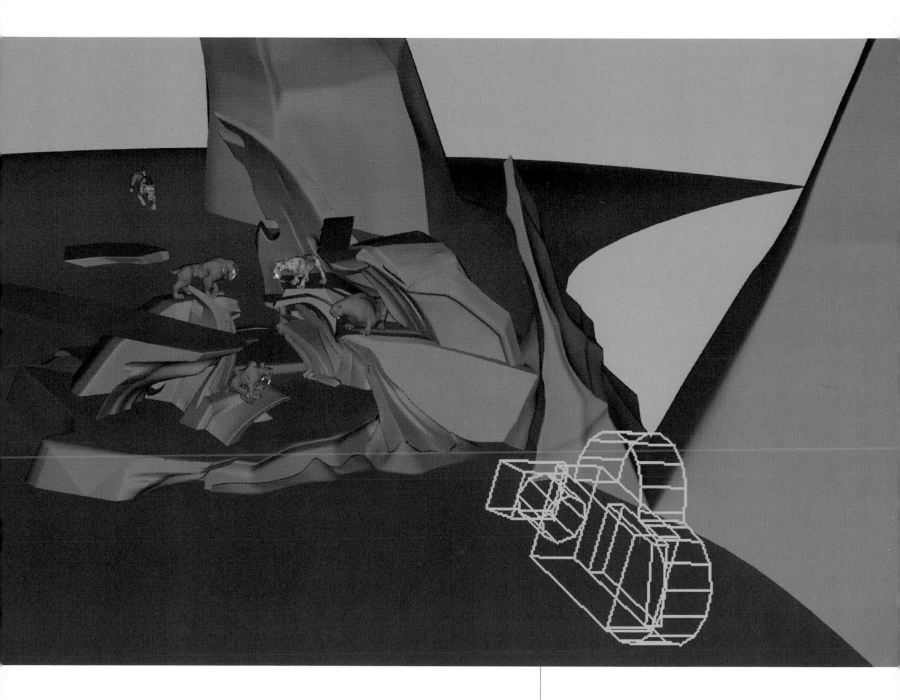

The primary concern of the storyboard artists is to tell the story effectively through images. The layout artists may find that when translated into 3D, the elements in the boards do not, or cannot, come together the way they are drawn. For example, layout may discover that between one shot and the next, a character must move too fast to be in the right position for the second shot. Either the set or the character position must be modified to solve the problem.

The 3D layout artist will not actually produce any final animation. Rough versions of characters are placed on the screen with only basic gestures and eye contact delineated. For example, if a scene calls for a character to walk from stage left to right, the 3D layout might

Here, the set seen on the opposite page is viewed from above. Note that the rock formations end just out of range of the virtual camera, whose position is indicated by a green outline. The ground has a strange bowtie shape because the modeler did not need to extend the set beyond what would appear in the final frame.

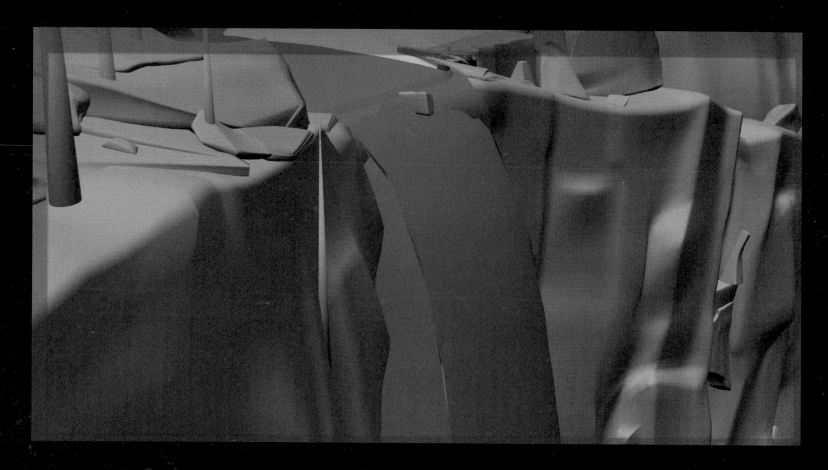

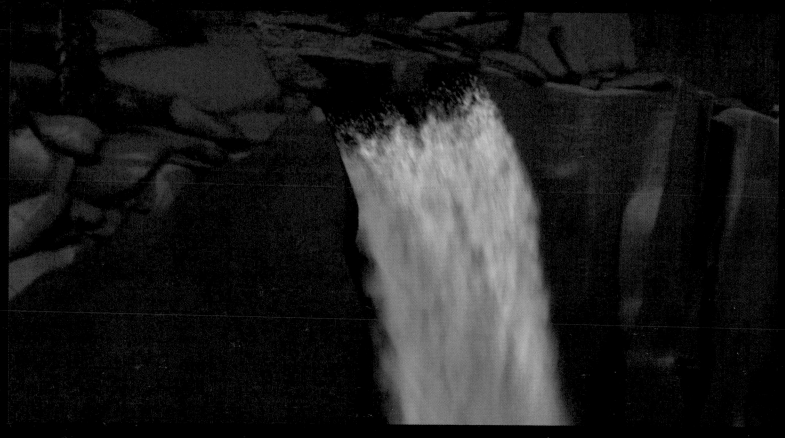

have the character slide across the screen to show the basic motion. 3D layout also places one camera into the scene file for each shot. Individual camera moves such as zooms and pans are roughed out, and all of the still or moving cameras are finalized.

When the layout is ready, each rough animation is reviewed in a large first-pass meeting with more than twenty people, including director Chris Wedge and co-director Carlos Saldanha representing animation. It is revised according to their comments and then reviewed in a second-pass meeting. At this juncture further refinements are made. The 3D layout is usually approved in a smaller third-pass meeting.

After approval, the animated 3D layout files are prepared to be sent to the other departments. Blue Sky Studios developed custom software called Breakout to help streamline production at this stage. Breakout works within Maya to calculate all of the geometry that is seen by a camera in a specific shot and then generate a file with that one camera and only the geometry that is in view. By discarding all of the parts of the model that are not necessary for the shot, the file sizes become much smaller and easier to work with.

Even though each shot is "broken out" into its own file, the modelers do not need to create or import a new model for each shot. Instead, Blue Sky "references" the models throughout production. With referencing, the models are not actually part of the scene file in Maya. Instead, Maya uses file names to point to files, which are then imported into the appropriate position. Think of a web page with links. When you click on a link, you are calling the address of another computer file that comes up in your web browser. You can make changes to linked files, and as long as they have the same name and are in the same place, the link is not broken. With referenced files in Maya, the set and characters can be updated throughout the production without recreating animations or scenes.

Before the animators start working on a shot, a technical director checks all of the geometry for accuracy and to make sure textures can be applied without problem. The geometry is broken down into priority models (which includes everything that comes in contact with the characters) and secondary models. At this point, the value of referencing becomes clear. Priority models are sent back to the modeling group for detailed final modeling, since the animators will need them to be highly finished. The secondary models have less geometry and less complex mapping, which reduces file sizes for the animators. The animators work with a combination of priority and secondary models to reduce file size and production time. The modeling department can produce final versions of the secondary models while the animators work with their low-resolution counterparts. When the animations are approved, the entire file is sent to assembly, where high-resolution versions of the entire set are imported into the file, and all of the surfaces are texture mapped.

OPPOSITE: A 3D layout is produced for every single shot of the movie. In the two stages of production seen here, the water and cliffs were first blocked out by the 3D-layout team; the technical directors and modelers then created a waterfall and set that matched the proportions of the 3D layout.

UNLIKE PAINTED BACKGROUNDS, COMPUTER-GENERATED SETS CAN BE DESIGNED TO be viewed from a variety of camera angles and different points of view. traditional cel animation and the matte paintings occasionally used in live-action filmmaking are flat. A flat background limits camera movement to a pan, zoom, or a still (or "locked down") shot. The CGI artist, on the other hand, has the option of utilizing flat backgrounds, fully realized 3D environments, or a combination of the two.

For *Ice Age,* says Chris Wedge, Blue Sky "tried to create a world that was not real, yet believable and somewhat familiar. It should have a logic and detail that is consistent. However, it is still a stylized place that is not reality." The task of inventing the look of this cohesive and compelling fantasy world fell to production designer Brian McEntee.

McEntee and his crew first developed their look for *Ice Age* on paper. (They worked in color from the beginning in order to address the integral issues of lighting and color palettes.) Once the director approved the set-design sketches, they were sent to the 3D-layout department. As we have seen, the 3D-layout team produced rough three-dimensional sets inside the computer, trying to match the hand-drawn images as closely as possible. If the camera was to be locked down to a single still shot of a particular set, the 3D artist "cheated" a little bit and made only the elements and parts of objects that would be seen from that view. If the scene was complex, with many different camera angles, the set would be a more fully realized 3D environment.

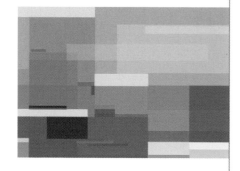

A color palette for each scene is prepared to serve as a guide for the lighting and materials artists.

For the next step, the 3D-layout artists printed out images of the sets that corresponded to the original sketches. Environmental designer Peter Clarke used these printouts as templates to create detailed line drawings. He might specify the kind of rocks and trees to be used in a particular scene, as well as the shape of the terrain. The concept sketch, 3D-layout files, and set-design drawings were then sent through the production pipeline to be modeled, textured, and lit. If the setting could be achieved with a matte painting rather than a 3D-model, it was sent to the digital matte artists. In most cases, a full 3D set was needed, and specialists such as set dressers were included in the production pipeline.

Digital matte artists work in a very different manner than their traditional film counterparts. Most of the matte paintings used in *Ice Age* depict broad vistas where the characters were relatively small and the camera was constrained to very little movement. Instead of painting these backgrounds on a large piece of glass, the digital artist combines dozens of rendered 3D images with his own 2D art, using Adobe Photoshop software. The resulting picture is "rendered out" in many layers. For example, in a landscape, a hill, the trees resting on top of it, the shadows of the trees, the brush and vegetation, the rocks, and the snow on the ground, may each be rendered in a separate layer. Thanks to this technique, the matte artist can work on one part of the image without affecting the other elements. For example, he might make the trees a little greener or blurrier without changing the ground color. It is just

In addition to the story-boards, paintings are pre-pared in pre-production to help visualize the scenes in the film. One by Brian McEntee, above, shows a scene that takes place in a natural "hot tub." The final render of the establishing shot of the hot tub scene as it appears in the film, left, follows McEntee's painting closely.

This vista from *Ice Age*, right, was created using a combination of 3D models and 2D digital painting. The artist digitally combined more than twenty layers to give the image the depth of a 3D render and the feel of a traditional 2D painting. Different layers are illustrated above.

like drawing with a cutout paper stencil: you can work in the area exposed by the stencil without worrying about messing up the rest of the painting.

For the creators of *Ice Age,* no virtual set was complete unless touched up by the set dresser. In live-action filmmaking, a set dresser is responsible for adding or removing items that make the environment more believable or less anachronistic. For example, in a bedroom set, the set dresser might add an alarm clock, a glass, and some pocket change on top of the night table to make it look as if someone lives there. In 3D, a set dresser will add small details that help create the illusion of a fully realized world. Things like a random handful of pebbles at the base of a boulder and a patch of grass at the foot of a tree help the audience view the set as a believable place. The set dresser does not alter the overall composition. He or she will just add small changes that enhance the original vision.

Even with all of the incredible talent at Blue Sky Studios, there is a great deal of "up and back" to produce the final animated images from the original production design sketches. McEntee, working under the direction of Chris Wedge, monitors the process from start to finish to make sure the film has a consistent look. As McEntee states, "It's like conducting music. You don't play all the instruments yourself, but you know how the music should sound."

Attention to subtle detail can make a big difference. After each scene is modeled and animated, the file is sent to a set dresser who will add finishing touches like rocks and clumps of grass that give the scene a more natural look. Below, a rendered scene from *Ice Age* before set dressing. Opposite, the scene shown as it will appear in the final film, with topographic detail added to the surface of the plateau.

EVERY SURFACE OF EVERY VISIBLE OBJECT IN CGI HAS TO HAVE A TEXTURE. A SURFACE

texture can be almost anything, from a simple, flat shade of color to a complex organic pattern like tree bark or a forest floor. At Blue Sky, the textures that cover surfaces are called materials. Materials are also known as shaders, depending upon the brand of software used. There's a great deal more involved in accurately describing a material than just its color. For instance, take a white object. If it's a cue ball, it will have a very smooth off-white surface that is somewhat reflective. If it's a handkerchief, it will be brighter white with a little texture for the weave. Frosted glass can be white with reflective and translucent properties. If the frosted glass is part of a light bulb, the issues of luminance, iridescence, and ambient light may come into play. The possibilities are endless. A technical director working with materials in CGI will usually study the way surfaces react to light in reality and then try to emulate those properties in the computer. Often, a big studio like Blue Sky will have an online library of materials that have been developed over years. It might include many different types of rock, wood, or glass, and other common materials. A technical director can then create a new material based on one or a combination of existing files.

There are two different methods of creating materials in CGI. One is known as procedural (or fractal) mapping. For a procedural material, the image is made from a mathematical formula. In a simple example, imagine a mathematical equation that says "draw a straight line, then at the end of that line, draw two lines at 45 degree angles that are half the width and length of the first line." This formula would make a "Y" shape. Imagine the next instruction was "repeat equation at the ends of new lines." The resulting image would look like a symmetrical tree with infinitely small branches at the ends. The viewer could zoom in to the end branches and there would be infinite, intricate detail. This is called a fractal image. Now, imagine that there was a slight random factor to the equation (something like "draw a line at 45 degrees + or - 2 degrees), varying the angle and the length of lines at each division. The resulting image would look much more organic. By changing the variables slightly again, a different fractal image is created. If the formula were written to calculate the fractal in the X, Y, and Z coordinates, the resulting "tree" would not be a flat graphic but a pattern that filled space, a 3D fractal. Through trial and error, fractals can be created that generate patterns reminiscent of many surface textures, both natural and manmade.

Both 3D and 2D fractals can be used to texture computer models. A 2D fractal image can be made to cover the surface of a model. With a 3D (or solid) fractal, the texture is rendered when the surface of the geometry intersects the fractal in space. Imagine a 3D fractal that mimics the surface texture of marble. Then imagine a series of models of columns inside the fractal. If you "cut away" the fractal from the models, you will have a series of columns whose surface is covered with marble texture. Furthermore, each one will be subtly different than the others because the fractal pattern differs from place to place. If, instead, you were to cover each of the columns with the same 2D fractal, they would all be identical, while in reality the pattern in marble always varies. In *Ice Age,* most of the objects are tex-

OPPOSITE: In one scene, the human baby, Roshan, is nestled in a straw basket, top. The texture or "image" maps used to add color and texture to the basket model are shown below. From top, they are the color map, the bump map for the edge of the straw, the bump map for the shape of the straw, and the bump map for wood grain. The bump maps add the illusion of surface texture. You'll note that the flat image maps of the basket texture seem stretched at the top. Once they are applied to the basket geometry, the weave will look even.

tured using procedural materials, because they provide organic-looking textures that remain sharp even on the big screen.

Along with procedurals, the technical directors at Blue Sky Studios use a texturing method known as image mapping. Image maps are digital pictures that are imported into the 3D program. For example, you can scan a picture of yourself, save it in the right format, import it into a 3D program, and then apply it to a piece of geometry like a sphere. The resulting image will not be a model of you; it will look like a picture of you wrapped around a ball. Image mapping is often used for photorealistic animations. The artist can use a photograph of a real wall and place it on simple geometry rather then recreating the complex texture of a wall in 3D. The artists in *Ice Age* used image mapping sparingly. Most of the time, image maps were associated with props for the human characters to give them a "manmade" look. A simple basket is a good example. Of course, it's not so simple: three associated bump maps were combined with a color image. A bump map creates the illusion of bumps on a flat surface. In the areas where the bump map is dark, the surface will appear to recede. Lighter areas appear to pop up. Since the bump map does not use color information, a grayscale—or black-and-white—image is all that is needed. Bump mapping is kind of like a trick. The actual model of the basket stays very simple, it just has the illusion of folds and bumps.

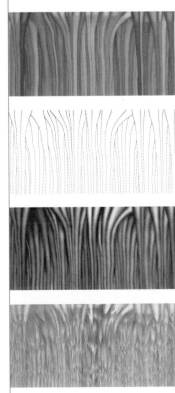

Two particular shots in *Ice Age* were an especially interesting challenge in texture mapping for the technical directors. They required the same exact set to be shown in broad daylight and then at night during a torrential rainstorm. Before the technical directors started adding textures, Dave Esneault, the lighting lead, positioned lights in the set so the artists would have an idea of the intensity, direction, and color of the lights, and how that would affect their work. To simulate a rainstorm in a live-action shoot, the production team might have just changed the lights and sprayed the set with water. Unfortunately, it's not that simple in CGI. Almost all of the materials had to be changed. When water absorbs into a material, it appears darker. If water is not absorbed, it may sheen over the surface, causing there to be specular highlights on a surface that was once dull. Light also bends as it passes through water. The amount that the light bends is known as the index of refraction. When a technical director makes a water texture, it is almost totally transparent. Therefore clear water is made visible by its reflective, specular, and refractive qualities. In the night shot, almost all of the textures were modified to make them appear darker and wet. Great care was taken to make sure the different textures were readable in the dimly lit scene. Even the texture on the animals' fur was changed to give their coats a matted look with a sheen of water. Since the scene takes place in an active rainstorm, the puddles on the ground would look lifeless and fake if the drops did not affect them. One of the technical directors at Blue Sky, Colin Thompson, created a custom script that generated an animated fractal texture to simulate circular ripples on the surface of the puddles. This animated texture was added to the ground material. In the final animation, the ripples are random and do not correspond to actual drops, but the overall effect is stunning and convincing nonetheless.

OPPOSITE: Sid stands his ground in dry weather, top, and during a rainstorm, bottom. The set is the same, but the colors and textures are considerably different.

A frame from the animated "ripple map" used to make it look as if raindrops are splashing into puddles on the ground in the rainstorm.

The fine ridges that create the appearance of windswept cliffs in this shot are an example of procedural, or fractal, mapping of textures. Since the texture map is only skin deep, the larger cracks and outcroppings in the rock were made by altering the model of the cliff.

In a giant cave, Sid inadvertently walks by his own evolutionary lineage frozen in the ice. The wall is textured with a combination of procedural maps of the surface of the ice and image maps of Sid's forebears. Note how the texture on the ice is varied so it appears to have cracks that are refracting light from different angles.

ANYTHING THAT IS DIGITALLY GENERATED OR ALTERED IS CONSIDERED A SPE-
cial effect in the live-action film industry. So technically, everything done by a computer
animator can be called a special effect. In the CGI field, however, there are certain kinds
of animation that are best achieved through specialized simulations rather than traditional
posing of characters. This is sometimes known as special-effects animation. Specifically,
flowing water, fire, smoke, blowing grass and leaves, rain, and snow are all varieties of special-effects animation. At Blue Sky, the technical directors are responsible for creating all
of the special effects, which require artistic talent, technical skill, and a tremendous
amount of hard work.

A great deal of special-effects animation involves dynamic simulations and particle effects.
A dynamic simulation is a kind of recreation of the Newtonian laws of motion inside the computer. For a dynamic simulation of a bouncing ball, for example, the technical director would
assign the properties of mass and velocity to a ball. The technical director can then assign a
specific gravity to the scene. Aside from the initial placement of the ball, the technical director
would not need to manipulate the object. He would need only to run the simulation and the
ball will bounce along a ground plane. Dynamics is not a very efficient way to make an animation of a bouncing ball, and most animators would rather create the animation by hand.
However, imagine an animation of dozens of marbles spilling out of a bucket. It would be
much easier to let the computer run a dynamic simulation than to animate it yourself.

Now imagine that the animator is spilling a bucket of sand rather than marbles. The tiny
grains of sand form a stream of dots flowing out of the bucket. Some of the grains might
swirl around in the air, some might stick to the bucket, but most would pour out in a
slightly random manner. In CGI they would be created using a particle effect, where rather
than being modeled, the grains of sand are emitted as particles from the bucket. In the
computer file, particles are represented by a single point in space. When the software does
the final render, they are assigned a texture so they have volume and can be seen.

The technical director can vary such attributes of the particles as lifespan (how long they
stay on screen before they disappear), speed, weight, and density. Certain parts of the
geometry in the scene will be designated as collision objects. A collision object is a 3D
object that will react to other objects or particles. Imagine that sand is pouring out of the
bucket and only the ground plane has been set as a collision object. Some grains will hit
the ground and bounce back and through the bucket. To fix the problem, the technical
director might make the inside bottom of the bucket an emitter and its other surfaces collision objects. To create a more believable animation, the technical director might incorporate friction into the scene. With only gravity applied to the particles in the above example, the particles would fall out of the bucket and bounce around the ground as if it were
a trampoline. By applying friction to the ground, the particles would "stick" more and
might just roll around in a more natural manner.

OPPOSITE: In CGI, snow and
wind, top, are special effects.
In *Ice Age*, the snowflakes
are actually pictures of
snowflakes on cards. The
forces of wind and turbulence
are assigned to the cards to
make them blow through the
air. Diego's fur also consists
of cards that bristle in the
wind. Flowing water, bottom,
calls for dynamic simulation
using partical effects.

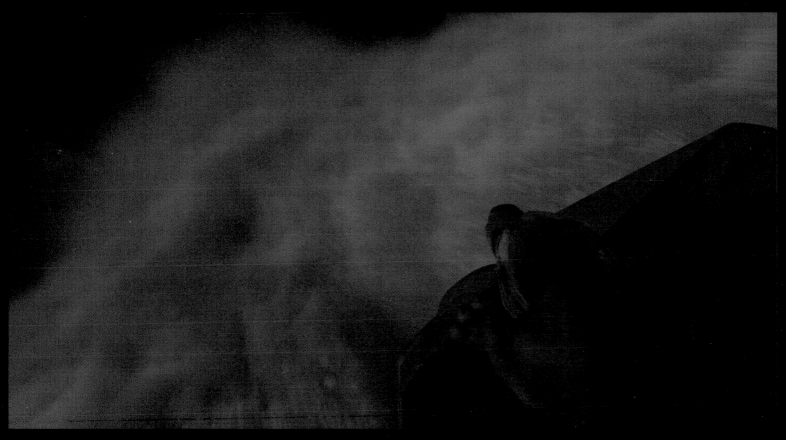

If the technical director wanted the particles to act like fire, he might set the gravity to a negative value, making the particles "fall" up, and then he would vary the lifespan of the particles so they would dissipate in a seemingly random manner. He would then attach a glowing transparent texture to the particles. If the technical director wanted the particles to act more like water, he would give them an infinite lifespan and then might set them to have a tendency to adhere to each other (just like real water, which has the properties of adhesion and cohesion). In CGI, particles that stick together are known as "blobbies."

For *Ice Age,* almost every scene in the movie required some kind of special effect. Whether it was a subtle light snowfall, wind rustling through the trees, or more spectacular waterfalls and volcanic eruptions, the artistry of the technical directors is evident in every final frame. In one incredible scene, for example, the main characters are surprised by a volcanic eruption underneath a giant glacier that leaves them stranded on a precarious ice bridge. First, steaming geysers burst around the unsuspecting characters. Next, melting ice crumbles away around them to reveal a river of rapidly flowing lava. While the scene is only on screen for 185 seconds (4,441 frames), it took 15 technical directors more than 2,835 working hours and 22,579 lines of custom code to complete.

The geysers were created using particle effects. The particle effects in each geyser were organized into four separate groups. Each group was in its own layer in the computer file, so that the properties of one could be changed without affecting the others. The first layer of the geyser simulated the initial blast of matter, with ice chips flying through the air as the steam penetrated the surface. The other three layers were organized like concentric tree rings. The inner core had very fast moving particles that shot relatively straight into the air. The next layer had slightly slower particles that sprayed out more from the center. The outside layer formed a ring around the base of the geyser that simulated heavier or lower velocity particles swirling closer to the ground. To make the particles look like a full column of three-dimensional steam rather than a bunch of fast moving dots or blobs, Maurice van Swaaij wrote custom code to utilize something known as "voxels." With voxels, the particles render as if they had thickness. The voxel technology also controls how the particles behave. If the particles are sufficiently close, they will interact more actively so the steam will appear more cohesive. If the particles are far apart, the steam will have a wispy look. The technical directors saved themselves a great deal of time and headache by using the same geyser many times throughout the scene. By making minor adjustments to the color and scale and then rotating the duplicates so different sides face the camera, no one is the wiser.

To make the swirling river of lava, the technical directors used special effects to modify a model inside the computer. They started with a flat NURBS plane for the model of the lava. John Turner, a senior research associate, wrote a piece of custom software called Swirl 2D.

OPPOSITE: The spectacular "ice bridge" sequence from *Ice Age* required many special effects. In the top two frames, particle effects animation simulates geysers of superheated steam as they burst through the ice. In the bottom two frames, a river of molten lava leaves Manny, Sid, and Diego stranded on narrow pillars of ice. The lava was created through an animated simulation of fluid dynamics. Overleaf, the ice bridge carved by the lava is seen in a long shot that requires special effects to simulate steam, lava, smoke, fire, and falling ice.

Swirl 2D calculates the theoretical flow of fluids around solid objects. It then generates a series of pictures based upon those calculations. For the lava effect, the software generated color, glow, bump, and gray-scale "displacement" images. The gray-scale displacement image (or map) has white areas that represent the crests of waves and darker areas that represent the troughs (think of a black-and-white topographical map). The gray-scale map was applied to the flat NURBS plane with another piece of proprietary software called Implicit Surfaces. Implicit Surfaces actually deforms the geometry to correspond to the gray-scale values of a 2D picture. It is kind of like having software that turns a flat map into a relief map. When you animate that map, you get three-dimensional waves ebbing and flowing across the surface.

Dynamic simulations are not limited to particle effects and bouncing balls. The same forces of gravity, friction, initial velocity, and turbulence can be used to alter the shape of a 3D model. If a model is set to deform due to forces in a simulation (like a flag blowing in the breeze), it is known as a soft body. For soft bodies, the vertices on the surface are given the properties of particles. The dynamic forces then affect those particles, and the surface of the model is "dragged along" with the movement of the particles. To keep soft bodies (like billowing flags) from stretching out of shape, the original object can be made into a target shape: the soft body has a tendency to snap back to that shape. Think of cafeteria Jell-O. If you move your dish, a rectangular slab of Jell-O will jiggle (or deform) while maintaining its volume. Eventually, it stops wobbling and returns to its original (or target) shape. Many computer animators use soft bodies (or similar dynamic tools like Maya Cloth) to animate clothing on CGI characters. In a cloth simulation, the body of the character becomes the collision object with the "soft body" clothing attached to the model. If the character were to move an arm quickly, the sleeve would wobble and deform in a manner similar to real cloth. This is known as secondary animation.

While a dynamic solution can be quite effective to represent secondary animation in clothing, it is extremely processor intensive. It will slow down both the animation and rendering process. For *Ice Age,* Blue Sky used its proprietary software called Follow Through instead. Follow Through is like a simple rubbery IK chain that is affected by the motion of the character. For example, if Follow Through was used on the tail of a cat, the tail would bounce as the cat walked. Since applying Follow Through to one of the characters is more of a rigging issue than a dynamic simulation, it is usually set up by the riggers at Blue Sky. This tool gives the animators greater control over the motion of soft objects. It is also much easier to use than a full dynamic cloth simulation.

Complex dynamic simulations require a great deal of processing power and technical know-how. As processors become more powerful and software becomes more sophisticated, more filmmakers are using these tools to create spectacular special effects through computer animation.

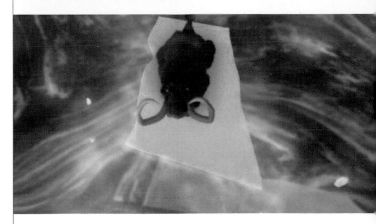

ONE OF THE MOST DIFFICULT THINGS TO DO IN 3D IS TO CREATE CONVINCING HAIR AND fur. One solution for creating hair, for example, would be to actually model and duplicate the individual strands. It would take literally thousands of modeled strands to make the character look like it has a thick head of hair. This would make for a very "heavy" or data-intensive model. There would be more geometry in a character's hair than the entire body. If the artist wants the hair to move (or flow) as the character moves, it creates another difficult obstacle. All of those thousands of strands of hair would have to be set so they bounce and move in the same general direction without colliding with each other. Instead, most animators use one of two solutions for fur: a card system or volumetric rendering of particles.

Three full-time technical directors worked for nine months on animal fur for *Ice Age*. Dave Walvoord, senior technical director, developed the card system Blue Sky Studios uses for short fur. It was first used for a mouse in the feature film *A Simple Wish* and then later in *Star Trek: Insurrection* for a photorealistic, yet otherworldly, hummingbird that seemed to have thick coat of feathers. To give the bird this coat, the technical directors started by mapping pictures of feathers onto simple geometric shapes. The texture maps of the feathers were overlaid by opacity maps that made the surface transparent wherever there was not a

These images depict the card system for fur as it was applied to the scrat. Top, the model covered with a green and blue image map that controls density of fur. Above, many of the thousands of cards that are needed to simulate fur, with color added to make them visible. Below, three of the clumps of fur that are pictured on the cards. Opposite: The scrat as he appears in the film, sporting his thick coat of virtual fur.

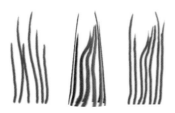

This is the "hummingbird" that Blue Sky created for the feature film *Star Trek: Insurrection.*

picture of a feather. Think of a painting on a perfectly clear piece of glass. If there is no reflection, the painting appears to float in the air. Thousands of these little panes of glass (or cards) were attached to the surface of the bird. For some shots, however, the bird was viewed at an angle where the viewer might see the edge of the cards, and the illusion would breakdown. To compensate, some areas of the bird were covered with tiny cones with images of feathers. The cones could be viewed from multiple angles without destroying the illusion that the bird was in 3D. The technical directors worked to perfect this technique for fur shading while producing *Bunny, Fight Club,* and, eventually, *Ice Age.* For *Ice Age* most of the cones were replaced by cards.

The technical directors apply fur onto a character using a 3D paint program for fur developed at Blue Sky. The technical directors paint with a virtual brush on the 3D model to determine the color, length, thickness, density, shadow, highlight, and specular attributes of the fur. Each of these attributes can be modified using separate image maps, which are laid on top of one another to create the final image. For example, a grayscale map controls the length of the fur. Completely white areas allow for the maximum fur length, while black areas are ostensibly bald. The gray values in between provide gradual variance. When that map is combined with a density map, the technical director can achieve thousands of per-

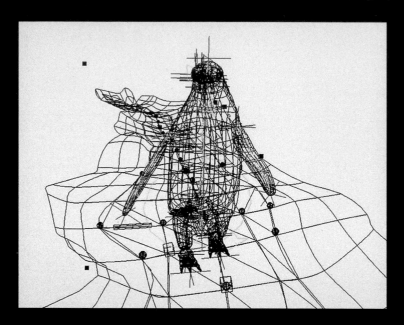

mutations of thickness and density. The fur program will also automatically generate slight random variations in fur color and density to give the fur a more natural, organic feel.

Even though the card system saves time and reduces memory consumption and render time by combining fur into "clumps" on cards, it still generates an impressive amount of geometry. The character of Diego, a saber-toothed tiger, needed more than 20,000 cards for a full coat of fur. Since most of the cards are 2D and they do not completely cover the surface, there are some angles where the viewer may see through the layers onto the underlying geometry (or skin). Blue Sky Studios utilizes a clever proprietary tool known as NURBS March to generate an image map (or digital picture) of the actual fur and apply it to the underlying character model geometry. If the audience sees through the cards that make up the fur, it sees a picture of more fur underneath. This creates the illusion of a very dense, thick coat. NURBS March works exceedingly well because of the way we naturally perceive the depth of a texture: our eyes are easily fooled when we are looking straight at it. A character's silhouette provides us with stronger visual cues as to the thickness and length of its fur.

To reduce the complexity of the geometry and generate smaller files that animate and render faster, the technical directors vary the level of detail (LOD) of the fur materials dependent upon the proximity of the model to the camera. The further away from the camera the character is, the less detail is necessary. The number of cards used to describe their fur is reduced for secondary characters that are in the background and even for the main characters when they are rendered at smaller sizes. LOD is determined (automatically) or at the discretion of the technical director.

To visualize how the volumetric system works, think of fireworks. When a rocket explodes, thousands of sparkles are propelled outward through the air, leaving trails behind them. As they get further away from the source of the explosion, they grow dimmer and eventually disappear. Although the sparkles travel in all directions, they are still subject to the forces of wind and gravity. For a CGI volumetric rendering, an emitter is similarly made to release a spray of particles, but their paths are rendered as solid geometry. Instead of trails of sparkling light, they describe tubes that look like strands of hair. The thickness and stiffness of the hair can be set to decrease along the path, just as the firework trails burn dimmer at the ends. And since this hair is generated as a dynamic effect, it can be subject to forces just like an active soft body.

Blue Sky Studios utilized a proprietary volumetrically rendered particle-based system for long, flowing human hair in *Ice Age*. A unique feature of Blue Sky's volumetric hair is that it is self-shadowing. This means that the individual strands of hair cast shadows on each other as well as the modeled surfaces. This creates a photorealistic image with depth and volume. Proprietary render algorithms speed up the processing times for the shadowing to make the feature practical for production.

OPPOSITE: Blue Sky produced a photorealistic penguin for the 1999 film *Fight Club* using its proprietary card system for feathers. The top left image shows the penguin in wireframe mode. The image to its right has color, but no texture. The bottom image shows the complete penguin with feathers.

BLUE SKY STUDIOS EMPLOYED ABOUT TWENTY-FIVE FULL-TIME CHARACTER ANIMATORS
on *Ice Age,* many of whom have previous experience in art, filmmaking, traditional 2D animation, or stop-motion animation. Character animators are often thought of as the actors
in an animated film. It is their job to combine body movement, timing, and facial expression to give each model an individual character.

The animators are led by the animation director, Carlos Saldanha. During the production of *Ice Age* it became evident to Chris Wedge that the director's job was "too much
for one person," and Saldanha was promoted and credited as co-director. Carlos
"shares the same aesthetic," says Wedge. The character animators at Blue Sky Studios
begin production of each sequence with a kickoff meeting where the directors explain
the action and motivation. Each sequence is then assigned a sequence supervisor who
focuses on production and coordination for the group of shots. The animators are
organized in a flat hierarchy with just two or three leads. Unlike Disney, animators are
not assigned to a single character throughout production. Instead, they are free to animate entire shots by themselves, while the animation director assures continuity from
scene to scene. Although the work is divided on a per scene rather than character-cen-
tric basis, animators who show an affinity to a certain character or type of animation
may become informal specialists. Like actors, the animators are given some time to
analyze a character's motivation and flesh out details of a performance. Before touch-
ing the computer, many animators will draw a series of thumbnail sketches to fill in
the missing elements from the 3D layout and help realize the intent of the directors as
stated in the kickoff meeting.

Ice Age director Chris Wedge
acts out a gesture for the
animators during a sweat-
box meeting (sitting behind
him is sequence director
Mark Baldo). Opposite, the
scrat seems to mimic his boss.

In 3D computer animation the animator works like a puppeteer, in that the models are
posed by manipulating a series of controls that create a performance. Unlike traditional
hand-drawn or stop-motion (puppet) animation, the characters are not drawn or posed for
every frame. Instead the animator sets up a series of keyframes that specify when and
where in a particular sequence a character will hold a certain pose, and the computer will
then automatically calculate the motion in between each of the keyframes. Before beginning to animate a character, an animator will usually test the model with a simple animation like a walk cycle. A walk cycle is a series of steps where the character starts and ends
on the same pose. Because the movement is cycled, it can be repeated without the viewer
being able to identify the starting point. The animator will also take the character through
a run cycle, lip sync, and extreme pose tests.

Each day, each animator produces a flipbook (or low-resolution animation) of his or her
work. Depending on the stage of production, the flipbook can be anything from a group of
character keyframes to an almost-complete animation. The film's editors arrive very early
each morning to prepare the previous day's flipbooks (by adding sound, cutting the new
material in with existing shots, outputting video, and so forth) for the daily sweatbox

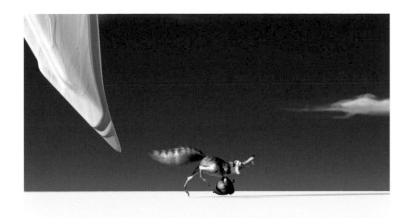

THIS SPREAD: The comedic opening scene of *Ice Age,* where the scrat tries to save an acorn from an onrushing avalanche, is a classic example of broad, exaggerated animation.

OVERLEAF: Frames from a more dramatic sequence requiring subtle animation: Nadia, holding her baby, Roshan, is trapped at the edge of a cliff by Diego. In the span of just a few seconds, and without saying a word, she expresses fear, tender love for her child, and determination.

Animation can be used to flesh out secondary characters. Although these aardvark-like creatures from *Ice Age* are almost identical, their different expressions (happy, cynical, dim) help to individuate them.

meeting. In the sweatbox, animators are given feedback on their work. During the day, the animation director also makes rounds, to work with the animators individually.

Maya is the primary software used for animation at Blue Sky and at most other professional 3D animation studios. An animator sets keyframes by moving a marker along a time slider to the frame—the exact point in time in a sequence—where he wants the keyed pose to be located; selects in turn the particular attributes of the character that he wants to animate; and sets a key for each one. This locks the position of the selected character attribute at that particular frame. It is important to note that a single character can have hundreds of parts and each part has dozens of attributes. Various attributes can be grouped so that they can be keyed together or selected individually. A few seconds of animation may contain hundreds or thousands of keyed attributes.

By default, the software will generate a spline motion path between keyframes. The spline path, like the default NURBS surface curve, will draw the smoothest path between a group of points. Suppose the task is to animate a bouncing ball. The animator might start by setting keyframes at the apex of each bounce and at the points where the ball hits the ground. Instead of making a straight path between each keyframe, however, the software would generate a smooth path that would look like a sine wave (or spline curve) between each keyframe. The resulting animation would be incorrect because the ball would spend as much time sliding along the ground as it does at the top of the bounce. To fix the problem, the animator would alter the path and timing of the bounce, so the ball moves faster as it drops, bounces realistically, and slows down at the apex of the bounce. To do this, the animators use a feature called the Graph Editor in Maya. The Graph Editor displays the path for every animated object in a scene. Each path has control handles at the keyframed points. By modifying the control handles, the motion of an object can be changed. To the uninitiated, the Graph Editor, with its multicolored intersecting curves, dots, and control handles, looks like an EKG for a very, very sick person. With some practice, working with the Graph Editor becomes second nature, and the animator is able to visualize the animation by the shape of the curves. To adjust timing for the overall animation, the animator will use the Dope Sheet tool within Maya. In the Dope Sheet is a grid, with the film's frames represented by the horizontal axis and the animated elements by the vertical axis. Using the Dope Sheet, the animator can easily move, delete, or "stretch out" a series of keyframes to change the timing of the scene.

The character models in *Ice Age*, with all of their complex surfaces, elaborate rigging, and detailed texture maps, are very "heavy," or data intensive. A heavy model is hard to work with and pose. Thanks to referencing, however, the character animators can use low resolution proxy models for their working files. The modelers prepare three models for each character: in low, medium, and high resolution. The lower resolution models were created from the originals by converting their NURBS surfaces into relatively simple 3D polygon shapes. The simplified polygonal model is bound to the same skeleton, but does not bend at the joints like the NURBS model. Instead, a model of a leg, for example, would be divided into two pieces, a thigh and calf, with an open space at the knee. The low resolution model is easier to move around the set and will provide the animator with a good idea of what the final model will do. The different versions can be toggled on and off within the same file.

The method of keyframing motion "by hand" used at Blue Sky Studios and other leading 3D animation studios is very different from a popular process known as motion capture. In motion capture a real actor is recorded performing the desired movements. Markers (either optical or magnetic) are placed on the actor's major joints. A series of cameras or magnets is carefully placed around the stage to record the position of each joint into the computer. The motion data is then brought into the animation software. The recorded motion of the actor's joints is assigned to the corresponding joints on a CGI character. The resulting animation will combine the performance of a real actor "in the skin" of a computer-generated creation. Motion capture will often have a kind of "floaty" look, because the character does not always appear integrated into the scene; it is similar in principle to a 2D technique known as rotoscoping. With rotoscoping, a real actor is filmed and then the frames are traced and colored in to look like they are hand drawn.

At the other extreme, some software comes with automatic walk and motion files that can be applied to models. In most cases, the default walk created using this automatic method plants the foot well, but the overall effect looks rigid and unnatural. Blue Sky keyframes every piece of character animation manually within Maya. There is more work to start with, in that there are no imported motion data or automatic animation functions. However, a custom set-up for each character provides a high degree of flexibility and, in the end, there is no substitute for a talented animator and hard work.

Of course, this kind of animation is time consuming. There are thousands of details involved in every shot. Whether it is a subtle movement of the eyes, or perhaps a shift in weight that gives the character more presence in a scene, an animator can tweak a single shot for weeks. However, the animators, like all of the production artists on *Ice Age*, are always kept to a strict schedule. As Mike Thurmeier, one of the animation leads, says, "You know you're done when they take it away."

The low-resolution model of Sid can be toggled on and off by the animators.

IN 3D COMPUTER ANIMATION EVERYTHING IS A SIMULATION. THE MODELS ARE SKINS THAT appear to be solid. The surfaces are "painted" with fractal designs that appear to be organic textures. The movement and the appearance of life in the characters is actually a series of carefully choreographed poses. Lighting is no different. Computer-generated lights are simulations of reality. How these lights are set up is partly dependent on the type of render software that will be used to produce the final frames of the movie, so lighting and rendering (explained in the next chapter) are closely related tasks.

The technical directors take great pains to achieve the natural lighting that a live-action filmmaker might take for granted. In reality, light from a single source (let's say a light bulb) will bounce from surface to surface, reflecting off some surfaces, partially absorbing into others, and eventually dissipating until it is almost imperceptible. If that bulb were placed in a white room with one wall painted bright red, the red wall would reflect red onto the other walls. This would give the room a slightly pinkish tint that would be very noticeable where the white walls meet the red. This phenomenon is known as light transfer.

In CGI, it's usually not possible to set up virtual lights and let them generate realistic light transfer off the models, because few computers have enough power to calculate the effects of light transfer, and so there is generally no light bounce in 3D computer animation. (Blue Sky Studios' own CGI Studio software, described on pages 82-83, is an exception to this rule, permitting bounced light thanks to its radiosity capability, but practicality dictated that *Ice Age* be lit in the more traditional manner.) Instead, a lighting technical director has to fake it. To simulate a light bulb in a white room with one red wall, he might set a virtual point light at the position of the light bulb. (A point is a light whose rays emanate out from a single point in space.) If it were an incandescent bulb, he would tint it yellow. He would simulate the effect of light bouncing off the red wall by adding a second, dimmer red "area" light pointing out from the wall. (An area light is a light that emanates from an area—like a rectangle—rather than a point.) In CGI, the emitted light, but not the actual light source, will show up in the final render. In the example above, the point light object and the rectangular area light object would be invisible; only the surfaces that they light are seen. A lighting technical director would need to add a special glow effect on the bulb to identify it as a practical light (as a visible light source is called in filmmaking). He would not add a glow effect onto the area light, since it is just used to simulate a bounce from the first source.

Blue Sky Studios employed twenty full-time lighting technical directors for *Ice Age*. In feature production, the lighting technical directors are involved relatively early in the process. Before the sets went to assembly for material development, David Esneault, the lighting lead, blocked out the lighting for the scene, enabling the materials artist to see the color, intensity, and angle of the light and shadow before texturing the geometry. When the sequence was textured and animated, it came back to the lighting technical directors. At

OPPOSITE: Just like in live-action filmmaking, lighting can set the emotional tone for a scene. An orange hued "magic hour" light and soft shadows add drama and beauty to a shot where Manny plays with the baby Roshan, top. The bottom scene, with its contrasting colors, bright light, and clearly defined dark shadows, emphasizes Manny's strength and power—an effect augmented by the low camera angle. Note how both the leaves and Manny's fur "pop" against the light blue sky.

Snow has its own unique semi-translucent and reflective properties, presenting an interesting challenge to the technical directors on *Ice Age*. Note how the light coming from the left of this shot creates soft, diffuse shadows because the surface of the snow reflects and diffracts some of the light. If you take a close look, you will see that even small areas like Diego's underbelly are relatively bright because the light bounces off the snow and transfers to his white fur.

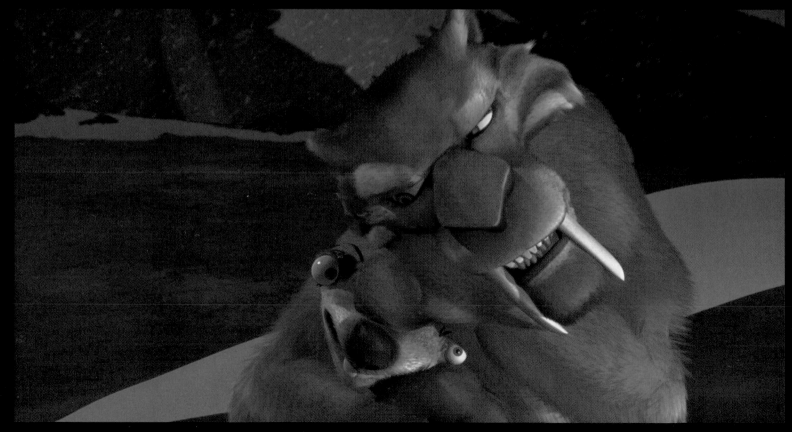

this point the lighting leads created a series of three or four master shots—called beauty frames—from the sequence, which were approved by the director.

Their task was complex. In a typical outdoor scene, for example, a technical director will start with a point light to simulate the sun. To keep the rays from the point light roughly parallel (like sunlight), it is placed very far away from the models and camera; it will likely be given a warm tone and set to cast shadows. To add detail into the dark areas, he will usually add a fill light—often another point light about half the intensity of the sunlight. The fill light is rarely set to cast shadows, because the fill is placed on the opposite side of the model from the sunlight. If the fill were to cast shadows, they would run contrary to the direction of the primary light source, giving the render an unnatural look. In the real world, however, infinite light transfer creates an ambient (seemingly directionless) light that does create soft shadows, which need to be added. To simulate light bouncing off the ground, the technical director will usually add a "ground bounce" ambient light. This light is often rather weak and it is not set to cast shadows. To add another layer of realism, a sky-light is often added. For example, if a scene has a blue sky, a soft blue ambient "sky light" will be placed into the setup to make the characters fit more realistically into the setting.

Once the sample beauty frames created by the lighting technical directors have been approved, the files move down the production pipeline to the render technical assistants, known as "render wranglers." A render wrangler's job consists of scheduling processing times, seeing the frames through the process, and then checking the final frames for anomalies. Anomalies may be in the form of intersecting geometry, lighting artifacts such as "flecks" of noise in a shadow, or, in some cases, the render just crashes. Wranglers are familiar with CGI Studio, Unix, and other specialized software so they can troubleshoot most problems without bouncing the work back to lighting technical directors.

Often, if a scene has very complex geometry, such as multiple characters and a detailed environment, the technical directors will break out different aspects of the scene to be rendered as separate layers, or "passes." If a character was rendered in a separate pass from the background, there would be one layer with the character silhouetted against black and another layer of the background without the character. A single shot may have many passes: background, mid-ground, and foreground layers; a character pass; shadow pass; specular or highlight pass; and dynamics or effects pass, as well as a depth pass. With the depth map, the technical directors can assign a blur to certain levels of gray that will emulate the limited focal range of real cameras. In reality, a close-up lens has a shorter depth of field than a normal lens. A telephoto lens usually has a longer depth of field. With a real camera, lighting conditions, shutter speed, and varying the aperture can also alter depth of field. Default 3D renders are more akin to how we actually see, with a universal sharp focus. However, in order to appear more "realistic," depth of field and, usually, even film grain is added to CGI to mimic the artifacts of traditional filmmaking.

OPPOSITE: Here are two frames from the same sequence. Note how the top frame evokes a cold, gloomy night, with its muted violet color palette. The dense snow effect is enhanced with volumetric fog that reduces visibility and diffuses the light. In the bottom frame, an off-screen fire emits a warm orange glow that illuminates Diego and Sid. Note that there is a special light linked just to the animals' eyes to give them a glassy, eerie glow without over-lighting their faces. This is an example of how 3D computer animation can offer advantages to lighting technicians not available in live-action filmmaking. With "light linking," the artist selects only certain pieces of geometry that are affected by the light.

AT BLUE SKY STUDIOS, AS WE HAVE SEEN, THE LIGHTING TECHNICAL DIRECTORS ARE RESPON-
sible for setting up the final render of each frame. A rendered frame is one in which the
models and sets are seen as they will look in the finished film. Rendering is complex
process whereby the virtual 3D scene, bathed in virtual light, is recorded by a virtual camera, and turned into a 2D image. It's what the studio's impressive render farm (see page
84) was set up to do. And it requires some industrial strength software as well.

Different render software uses different technical means of recording the "light" that is
gathered by the "camera." Blue Sky Studios' own CGI Studio uses raytracing. Raytracing
literally traces the rays of light from the objects to the camera (see page 82), and does an
effective job with transparency, reflections, specular highlights, and the representation of
surface materials. It is important to note that not all raytracing software is the same. Blue
Sky's proprietary raytracer handles the distribution of light in a more effective manner
than other commercial products. Using another rendering capability called radiosity, CGI
Studio can even take account of some of the effects of light transfer. *Bunny* was a break-
through in rendering because it showcased Blue Sky Studios' combination of raytracing
and radiosity rendering techniques.

Radiosity's key element is its ablity to calculate the transport of light from one surface to
another. CGI Studio uses first-order solution sampling. This means the renderer calculates
one bounce between surfaces. Second order would calculate two bounces, and so forth.
While CGI Studio can calculate the more accurate second- and even third-order sampling,
the render times would be impractical. In most cases, the second-order effect is too subtle
to be detected by the average viewer anyway, and it is usually more efficient to just add
another weak light source.

OPPOSITE AND BELOW:
These images are tests of the interior set used for *Bunny*. The first, opposite top, was rendered without using radiosity. As impressive as it is in its attention to detail and naturalistic quality, the test looked gray and some of the shadows appeared too dark and flat. After the first radiosity test was also thought to be a little bit dark, the lighting technical directors added a white card to bounce light down, below right, a technique that radiosity, with its ability to calculate light transport, makes possible. The final image, opposite bottom, is the set as it appears in the film, with radiosity and bounced light from the card. Note how the chrome handle on the stove reflects light upward and how the shadows under the faucet are softer and have color. It shows the subtle lighting effects that made the film so impressive to many experts.

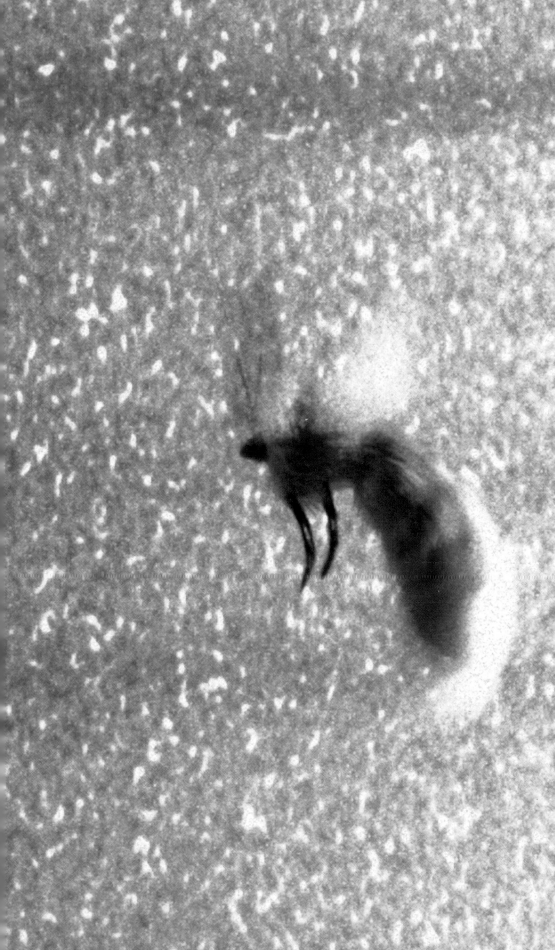

The end of *Bunny*, in which a fluttering moth beckons Bunny "home," is a tour de force of light and motion. The hazy blue light, the glowing halo around the moth, and the motion blur on the translucent wings of the moth were all created in 3D using Blue Sky's rendering software. Most animation studios would have tried to duplicate these subtle effects in post-production using 2D additions. Because Blue Sky generated the lighting effects in 3D using real light simulations, the end result is more convincing and realistic.

Radiosity does have the drawback of very slow render times. In *Bunny* the central character was rendered with raytracing, because all of the intricate shadows on her fur would have been impractical with radiosity. For *Ice Age,* the technical directors did not use radiosity to render any of the scenes since time was of the essence.

Occasionally, a scene calls for volumetric lighting effects to achieve the dramatic rays of light emanating from a practical source. Volumetric light is simply light that you can see. Think of a car headlight on a foggy night or light shining through the window of a dusty attic. In both of these real-world instances, the light is actually bouncing off tiny particles (water and dust), so the light appears to have volume. In CGI, volumetric lighting is not a particle effect. Instead, the technical director modifies the attributes of the actual light to render it volumetrically. In the final scene of *Bunny,* furry moths fly toward a volumetric light, all casting soft shadows. At the time *Bunny* was made, Blue Sky's render farm was not equipped to handle the incredible render times required to produce each frame. Compaq helped out with its own massive render farm.

At the end of the rendering process, the directors may still feel that certain sequences or shots are not as good as they could be. At this point, it is often faster to work directly on these frames with a digital-paint program—essentially doing 2D touch-up—than to send them back down the pipeline and redo them in 3D. This applies both to the clean-up of small errors and, even at this late stage, the creation of effects that are easier to produce in 2D than 3D. This final clean-up marks the completion of the technical tasks necessary to create the images for 3D animation. All that remains is the process of outputting the digital images to film that can be projected in theaters.

OPPOSITE: Bunny (top) was rendered with raytracing, because using radiosity would have taken too much time to process on the computer. Even so, with her bright eyes and glasses, she presents a tour-de-force of complex lighting and reflection. The climactic scene of *Bunny* (bottom) was rendered in CGI Studio. Compaq donated processing time on its own massive render farm to help Blue Sky complete the sequence process on the computer.

Although radiosity takes much more time to render, it saves a great deal of time when setting up the scene. For example, it enabled the lighting technical assistants to illuminate the entire porch light set from *Bunny* (left) with just one single practical light—the light bulb. It is remarkable how close the CGI image is to a photograph of a real porch light (above).

THE STEPS REQUIRED TO COMPOSIT 3D COMPUTER ANIMATION AND LIVE-ACTION FOOTAGE —a task at which Blue Sky excels—are somewhat different from what we have described. If live-action film is part of the mix, the goal is the creation of a seamless, photorealistic image incorporating animated digital models.

For compositing with live-action footage, Blue Sky uses Inferno, a custom high-end computer with software specifically designed for this purpose, manufactured by Discreet. One of the largest technical challenges of combining live-action film with digital special effects is working with high-quality film images in the computer. Inferno can perform real-time effects on uncompressed 2k (2048 x 1556 pixel) images. Most lower-end systems must use compression for real-time effects and therefore will degrade the quality of the image. After the digital work is done, getting the images out of the computer and back on film can be another technical headache. To combine CGI and live-action footage, the 35mm film is first scanned (or digitized) using a Kodak Genesis film scanner. Each of the frames is usually stored at 2k resolution. Occasionally, images are scanned at 3k or 4k, if only a portion of the frame will fill the screen or the images will be used for a large-screen projection like IMAX. Blue Sky sends the completed digital images for output on a high-end film recorder like a Kodak Lightning II using Cineon software.

A good example of high-end live-action compositing is the work Blue Sky did for the film *Alien Resurrection*. One underwater scene called for animated aliens to to swim into a live-action set and then for one of them to explode. The computer artists collaborated with the film crew on set to help plan the shot for transition to post-production. (Post-production refers to any work done after filming is complete. "We'll fix it in post," is a common solution in Hollywood.) While the modelers worked on the alien (see pages 24-25), the scenes were filmed with the knowledge that the models and the effects would be added in digitally. The crew took a still shot that served as the "clean plate," with just the set elements in the background. They also shot a full-sized model of a dummy alien exploding. Senior digital

THIS PAGE AND OPPOSITE: Steps in compositing live-action and CGI animation for a scene in *Alien Resurrection*. The first image shows a wireframe view of a model of a swimming CGI alien. Next, the untextured model of the alien is placed over the live-action background plate. Finally, the fully rendered, lit, and textured computer-generated alien is seamlessly composited with the live-action shot.

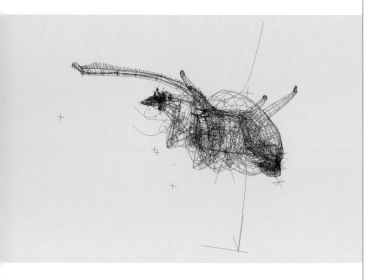

paint artist John Siczewitz removed wires and markers from the background plate. He then color-corrected the shot and added some digital bubbles. He repeated the process for the footage of the dummy alien and enhanced the explosion. The models were animated in SoftImage with an Alpha channel. An Alpha channel is a separate layer that is a grayscale silhouette for each frame of the geometry in a scene. The moving silhouette image is then used as a perfect-fitting mask to incorporate the digital images into the background. Live footage was used for reference and reflection maps. Using the Inferno, Siczewitz color-corrected the CGI aliens, added grain to make them look like they were shot on film, and composited in a soft shadow of the swimming aliens on the surfaces of the real set. For the explosion, the CGI alien in the background was replaced with the exploding real model, and the surface of the foreground alien was changed to reflect the bright orange flash of light. Once all of the elements were together, Blue Sky added a slight wobble into the camera to give the viewer the feeling of floating underwater. The resulting shot is a seamless and "believable" integration of live action, special effects, and CGI elements.

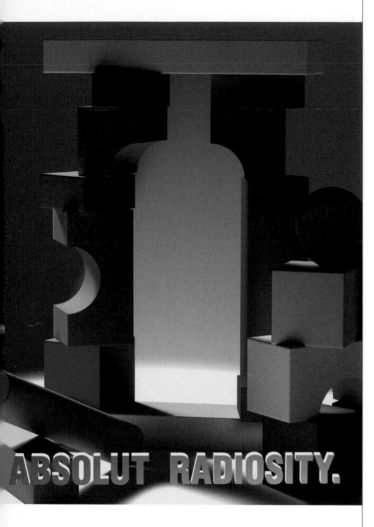

ABSOLUT RADIOSITY.

This parody of an Absolut ad was actually produced to test Blue Sky's CGI Studio rendering software. The colored blocks provide an excellent opportunity to see how realistically CGI Studio handles light transfer between colored objects.

WHEN BLUE SKY STUDIOS WAS FOUNDED IN 1987, COMMERCIAL CGI TOOLS WERE EITHER non-existent or in their nascent stages. Out of necessity, the company created its own proprietary renderer and other software systems. Today Blue Sky still uses the same core renderer—CGI Studio—it developed many years ago. CGI Studio has become the most sophisticated and arguably the best rendering software used in production anywhere. Eugene Troubetzkoy, Carl Ludwig, and Michael Ferraro were responsible for creating and implementing the rendering engine. Ludwig wrote the raytrace renderer. Troubetzkoy wrote the code that calculates the geometric intersection, and Alison Brown worked as a software architect. Troubetzkoy found that his work as a nuclear physicist was directly applicable to computer graphics. As he says, "In nuclear physics you follow neutrons. With 3D, you follow the light." Of course, it is slightly more complex than that. In CGI Studio there are approximately 80,000 lines of code to describe the geometry and another 19,000 in the renderer alone. The code is constantly changing to meet new challenges. Ludwig says, "One of the advantages we have over people who make commercial raytrace packages is that we are in production. It gives you tremendous insight into what is needed in order to effectively render extremely complex scenes. We can work on new problems every single day and it has created a symbiosis between production and research that is extremely healthy. It just doesn't get any better."

One of the most impressive features of Blue Sky's renderer is that it does not tessellate the geometry—that is, convert the surfaces into a pattern of interlocking polygons. All other commercial renderers convert NURBS surfaces into polygons before calculating texture and light. With tessellation, the software calculates the distance of the geometry from the camera and then displays enough polygons in order to simulate smooth surfaces. The closer the object, the more polygons. Tessellation uses up a great deal of RAM and, even if the renderer is working properly, there can still be "horizon problems" where the image will break down and show rough edges. CGI Studio reads the NURBS information directly, so that in theory the camera can get infinitely close to the geometry without its ever breaking down into flat surfaces.

CGI Studio uses raytracing rendering to create an image. It therefore handles light in a fundamentally more accurate and believable manner than the more common scanline technique. "Raytracing is intrinsically slow," says Troubetzkoy, but his team has written algorithms that speed up the calculations with very little loss of quality and so make raytracing practical for production. The software uses sampling to calculate the light emanating from an object, because it is impractical for the computer to calculate every ray of light. CGI Studio then interpolates between the points to render a complete image. Thanks to the power and speed of CGI Studio, Blue Sky Studios is perhaps the only large production facility to consistently use a raytrace render. "Raytracing is a different paradigm," says Ludwig. "It definitely does simulate the way light works in the real world better than a scanline renderer. As a result you can see the way light reflects off different materials more accurately. Having said that, all that it really does is broaden the gamut that you can achieve. It's not just about achieving reality. It is about giving things a dimensional quality and a richness that you don't normally get in simple rendering systems."

CGI Studio also has the capability of creating radiosity renders. With radiosity, each surface is treated as a potential light source. The intensity and color of the light from each surface is determined by direct and bounced light. When bounce lights are accounted for, the render takes on an incredible, photorealistic feel. Most radiosity renders tessellate the surfaces and then assign a value to the individual polygons. Blue Sky Studios has the only renderer that uses raytracing with the radiosity and reads in the true NURBS surface. The combination of these incredible technological elements makes CGI Studio unparalleled in the computer-graphics field. There was some thought about making the tool commercially available, but as Eugene puts it, "Not everyone needs a Rolls Royce. We'd be selling Rolls Royces."

While the R+D group constantly improves the CGI Studio rendering software, the team is also working on new and exciting special effects. Realistic flowing water, wind blowing through a characters' hair, plumes of fire, lava flows, and a myriad of other effects that push the envelope of computer-generated imaging are all made possible by the efforts of the R+D team. While the capabilities of the software become more and more impressive, the interface and usability becomes simpler so the artists and technical directors at Blue Sky Studios can be free to create anything that can be imagined.

This radiosity test shows four spheres, one of which is clear. The light reflects, refracts, and spreads around the image in a photorealistic manner.

A background used for a comical animated short called *Space Boy* was created using a mathematical formula known as a fractal algorithm. The only thing modeled in the scene is the space platform in the foreground.

IN THE BACK LOT OF A TYPICAL MOVIE STUDIO YOU WOULD EXPECT TO SEE CAMERAS, LIGHTS, sets, trucks, sound equipment, miles of cable, and a myriad of machines that support the filmmakers. The back lot of a digital production is a complex infrastructure of processors, switches, and servers that are off limits and out of view. The computer network described below is not part of any single step in the production process; it is literally the backbone of the studio, without which digital filmmaking would not be possible.

If you took a casual walk through Blue Sky Studios, you would notice that each person has a computer monitor, mouse, and keyboard on his or her desk, no different than most companies and certainly to be expected in a computer-animation production facility. What is not immediately apparent is that these workstations are networked to enough processing power to qualify the studio as one of the top supercomputing facilities in the United States. There are four people in the systems group who are responsible for a total of about 750 computers—more than four per employee. Andy Siegel, head of systems, is a computer scientist. The other members of his team come from varied business backgrounds. All display a natural affinity for troubleshooting technical problems.

The most impressive component of the network is the render farm, housed inside a glass-enclosed machine room. A render farm is a collection of computers connected through a high-speed network designed to handle the sorts of complex, processor intensive calculations necessary to produce a computer-animated feature film. Each computing task is divided into smaller "chunks," which are handled by single processors and then merged back into the whole. Unlike a mainframe computer, the render farm can be made more powerful by adding more, relatively inexpensive, servers. At Blue Sky Studios, the system consists of 512 Compaq servers mounted on seventeen rack modules. Each server has a single 616MHz Alpha processor. The Alpha chip is an incredibly fast RISC (Reduced Instruction Set Computer) microprocessor developed by Digital Equipment Corporation. A RISC processor differs from the processor in a typical desktop computer in that it breaks up calculations into many small tasks and processes them very quickly. The Alpha chip is one of the fastest processors on the market today. Each Compaq in the render farm has 1 gigabyte of RAM, more than ten times the amount of RAM in the average desktop computer, and a 10 gigabyte hard drive. The machines are running a Unix-based operating system called Tru64. Additional computing power is available in the form of five Silicon Graphics Origin 200 computers, one sixteen-processor Origin 2000, an eight-processor Onyx 2, and a quad-processor Onyx 2. The machine room is temperature controlled by specialized refrigeration units that generate sixty tons of air conditioning.

The network hardware consists of twenty-two 100baseT Extreme Summit48 network switches, each tied with a gigabit uplink to the extreme Summit7i switch with a capacity of 32 gigabit Ethernet ports, and a file server consisting of three Compaq ES40s. The

OPPOSITE: Blue Sky's temperature-controlled machine room, top, is the nerve-center of the studio. About half of the 512-processor render farm can be seen from this angle. Behind all of the neatly stacked racks of servers and switches is a waterfall of cables connecting more than 735 computers in a high-speed network, bottom.

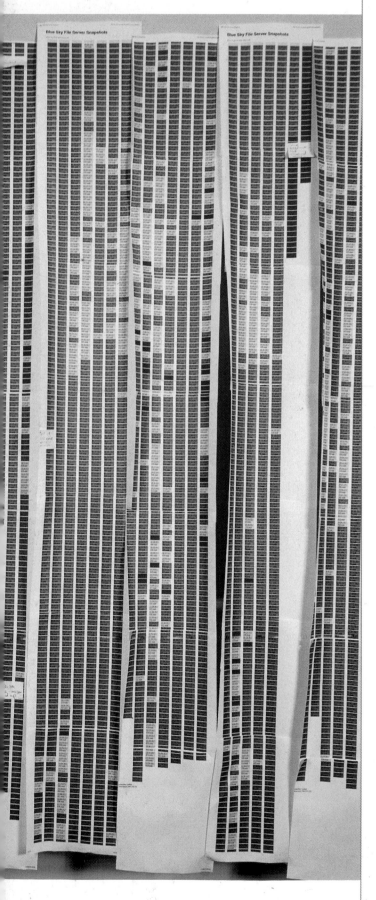

switches and servers store and route massive amounts of data to different addresses throughout the network.

In case of power failure, there is a 225-kilowatt UPS (uninterrupted power supply) back-up system, which can keep all of the computers running for a few minutes so they can be shut down without damage to the hardware or loss of data. The electricity to power all the "toys" in the machine room runs to $25,000 per month.

Most of the artists and technical staff at Blue Sky Studios use Silicon Graphics (SGI) work-stations. Each machine has at least one gigabyte of RAM, a 21-inch monitor, and a 9-giga-byte ultra SCSI hard drive. The workstations are a combination of O2 and Octanes with R12,000 MIPS processors. Individual workstation hard-drive space is less important because Blue Sky Studios has over 3.5 terabytes (that's 3,500 gigabytes) of accessible stor-age space online. This massive storage is backed-up to tape a few times a week. All SGI computers run the IRIX operating system, which is a form of Unix. Unix is usually the preferred operating system for professional computer scientists and administrators. It is extremely stable and allows for true multitasking. It is also an excellent system for running servers and adding custom scripts and user accounts. A few years ago, Unix was the only operating system used by high-end 3D artists. Today, most 3D-rendering software, includ-ing Maya, is available for less expensive Macintosh and Windows-based computers. Still, many professionals prefer the SGI systems.

The demands on the network are enormous. Many gigabytes of data are passed through the fiber backbone daily. A single user will typically access a few hundred megabytes of data during the workday. In some cases, the system must handle uncompressed digital video on demand, as well as file sharing by many dozens of simultaneous users. According to Siegel, the key to a smooth running network is to "keep it simple" and "use what works." Of course, what is simple to some can be rather daunting to the rest of us.

A chart hanging on the wall outside the machine room gives the systems people at Blue Sky a quick view of the entire network. The green squares represent workstations that are humming along fine. The yellow squares are com-puters that are having some problems. All of those red squares mean that somebody in systems won't get much sleep tonight.

ACKNOWLEDGMENTS

This book would not have been possible without the efforts of the many dedicated individuals. I would like to thank everyone at Blue Sky Studios who took time out during the incredibly busy production of their first feature film to answer questions and provide all of the information and stunning images in this book. Thanks to Virginia King, Kevin Bannerman, and the team at Twentieth Century Fox for their insight and support of this project. Thanks to Eric Himmel, Brankica Kovrlija, and their colleagues at Harry N. Abrams, Inc. Thanks to my colleagues and friends at New York University Tisch School of the Arts for providing a remarkable academic atmosphere that promotes both creative and scholarly pursuits, to John Canemaker for his invaluable mentorship and guidance, and to my wife Donna for her support, patience, and sacrifice that has made this book and my career possible.

—PETER WEISHAR

EDITOR: Eric Himmel
DESIGNER: Brankica Kovrlija

LIBRARY OF CONGRESS CATALOGING-IN-PUBLICATION DATA

Weishar, Peter.
  Blue sky : the art of computer animation : featuring Ice Age and
  Bunny / Peter Weishar.
      p. cm.
  ISBN 0-8109-9069-5
  1. Computer animation. I. Title.
  TR897.7 .W45 2002
  778.5'347—dc21

                                                    2001058988

Published in 2002 by Harry N. Abrams, Incorporated, New York
All rights reserved. No part of the contents of this book may be
reproduced without the written permission of the publisher.

Printed and bound in Italy

10 9 8 7 6 5 4 3 2 1

Harry N. Abrams, Inc.
100 Fifth Avenue
New York, N.Y. 10011
www.abramsbooks.com

Abrams is a subsidiary of

LA MARTINIÈRE
G R O U P E